PUBLISHED BY WELBECK CHILDREN'S BOOKS
An imprint of Hachette Children's Group
Part of Hodder & Stoughton Limited
Carmelite House, 50 Victoria Embankment, London, EC4Y 0DZ
An Hachette UK Company
www.hachette.co.uk
www.hachettechildrens.co.uk

An Hachette UK Company
www.hachette.co.uk
www.hachettechildrens.co.uk

DISCLAIMER

This book has not been authorised, licenced, or endorsed by Formula One Licensing B.V. or any other Formula 1 company. F1,
FORMULA ONE, FORMULA 1, GRAND PRIX and related marks are trade marks of Formula One Licensing B.V.. The book's content,
including names, characters, and events, is not officially endorsed or affiliated with the National Association for Stock Car
Auto Racing, MotoGP, World Rally Championships, DAKAR Rally, o r 24 Hours of Le Mans.

Active stats correct as of May 2025

10 9 8 7 6 5 4 3 2 1
ISBN 978 1 8045 3845 6

Printed and bound in China

Author: Alex Rice
Senior Commissioning Editor: Suhel Ahmed
Design Manager: Matt Drew
Picture research: Paul Langan
Production: Melanie Robertson
Consultant: Peter Higham

A catalogue record for this book is available from the British Library.

The authorised representative in the EEA is Hachette Ireland,
8 Castlecourt Centre, Castleknock Road, Castleknock, Dublin 15,
D15 YF6A, Ireland

PICTURE CREDITS
The publishers would like to thank the following sources for their kind permission to reproduce the pictures in this book.

Alamy Stock Photo: Associated Press 102B, Mariusz Burcz 87R (CLASSIC), James Cheadle 105, Michael Doolittle 98BL, Olrat 111B, Sipa US 104BR, WENN Rights Ltd 112TR

Getty Images: AFP 30, 90, Robert Alexander 56TR, 56BL, James Allan 85TR, David Allio/Icon Sportswire 61T, 95TL, 95TR, 95R, Michael Allio/Icon Sportswire 58-59, 94BL, Eric Alonso 24L, 75BL, Olivier Anrigo 75BR, Bruno Barros / DPI / NurPhoto 77T, Bettmann 63T, 64TR, 64B, Sam Bloxham/LAT Images 26R, 112B, Alexander Bogatyrev/SOPA Images/LightRocket 69BR, Matthew Bolt/Icon Sportswire 95L, Joe Brady 108-109, Jose Breton/Pics Action/NurPhoto 66-67, 74TR, 74R, 75BC, Frederic J. Brown/AFP 42TR, Jeffrey Brown/Icon Sportswire 63B, Bernard Cahier 18TR, 103R, Rudy Carezzevoli 39B, Alex Davidson 78-79, 78B, 79T, Carl de Souza/AFP 85C, Philippe Desmazes/AFP 87TL, Danilo Di Giovanni 75TC, Andrea Diodato/NurPhoto 24R, Neville Elder/Corbis 99TRL, Al Fenn 96R, Jonathan Ferrey 55TL, 65T, Franck Fife/AFP 86-87, GSI/Icon Sport 23TR, Simon Galloway/LAT Images 42-43, Sean Gardner 53B, Christophe Gateau/DPA/AFP 110L, James Gilbert 57TL, 61BR, 65R, Florion Goga 31R, Chris Graythen 25L, 52B, 56BR, 57TC, 57BC, 57BR, 64TL, Ralph Hardwick/Sutton Images 83BR, 84BL, Paul Harris 59BR, Anwar Hussein 29R, ISC Archives/CQ-Roll Call Group 51B, 56TL, ISC Images & Archives 46B, 97TR, 102T, Kym Illman 21B, Andrej Isakovic 16B, Dan Istitene/Formula 1 14-15, Jaguar Racing 40, Maurice Jarnoux/Paris Match 28L, David Jensen 52-53, Qian Jun/MB Media 25R, Keystone 29L, Todd Kirkland 44-45, 55B, Klemantaski Collection 28R, David E. Klutho /Sports Illustrated 101L, Ozan Kose/AFP 80-81, LMPC 96L, Robert Laberge 69L, LAT Images 85BL, Will Lester/Icon Sportswire 94L, Zak Mauger/LAT Images 8-9, 10-11, 27L, Matt McClain 97, McNeil/Sutton Images 19C, Hazrin Yeob Men Shah/Icon Sportswire 74BR, Vince Mignott/MB Media 26L, Ronald C. Modra 98-99, Vesa Moilanen/AFP 83TR, Jean-Francois Monier/AFP 89T, 91TL, 91L, Dean Mouhtaropoulos 87R (BIKE), 87R (TRUCK), 87R (QUAD), 87R (BUGGY), Meg Oliphant 57TR, Dario Oliveira/Anadolu Agency 100-101, Mike Owen 68-69, Octavio Passos 83L, Elliot Patching/Sutton Images 6-7, Valerio Pennicino 79BR, Doug Pensinger 104C, Emanuele Perrone 87TR (SSV), David Phipps/Sutton Images 91B, Larry Placido/Icon Sportswire 59T, 60-61, Daniel Pockett 38T, Joe Portlock/Formula 1 27R, 39T, Jakub Porzycki/NurPhoto 13, Mike Powell 95B, Racing Photo Archives 56TC, David Ramos 19BR, Logan Riely 46-47, Quinn Rooney 100C, Clive Rose 31L, Jean-Yves Ruszniewski/Corbis/VCG 19T, Chris Ryan/Corbis 101TL, Ronaldo Schemidt/AFP 82-83, Rainer Schlegelmilch 18BL, Marco Serena/NurPhoto 70-71, Patrick Smith 59BC, Andy Soloman/UCG/Universal Images Group 103L, Jeff Speer/LVMS/Icon Sportswire 94-95, Brian Spurlock/Icon Sportswire 62-63, 62BL, Matt Stone/MediaNews Group/Boston Herald 101R, Maarten Straetemans/AFP 76-77, Sutton Images 36L, 84C, James Sutton/Formula 1 38B, Jack Taylor 92-93, Michael Tee/LAT Images 18L, Noushad Thekkayil/NurPhoto 70L, Mark Thompson 16-17, George Tiedemann /Sports Illustrated 56BC, Jared C. Tilton 50-51, 54-55, 57BL, 58B, Jared C. Tilton/Formula 1 37T, Yoshikazu Tsuno/Gamma-Rapho 106-107, 111T, VCG 36-37, Bruno Vandevelde/Eurasia Sport Images 88-89, Hector Vivas/Jam Media/LatinContent 101TR, Steve Wobser 69R, 75TL, 75TR, Waleed Zein/Anadolu 110B

Shutterstock: Golden Sikorka 18-19, Punjab Bari 20-21, 22, top dog 84R, Winderfull Studio 23TL, 23B

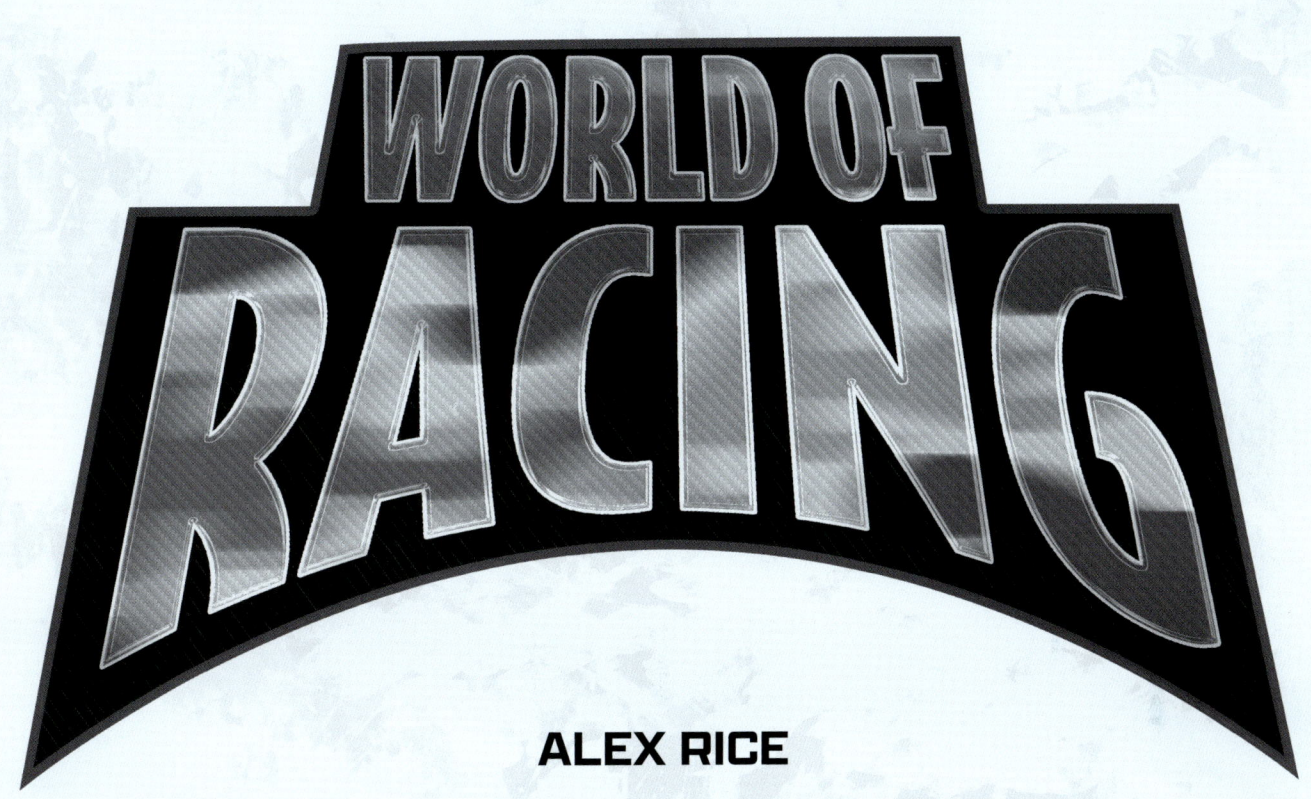

WORLD OF RACING

ALEX RICE

THE ULTIMATE GUIDE TO MOTORSPORTS AROUND THE GLOBE!

WELBECK
CHILDREN'S BOOKS

CONTENTS

Welcome to the World of Racing – a comprehensive guide to the sports, races, drivers, and of course vehicles that keep millions of us on the edge of our seats every year.

It takes a huge team effort to cross the line first, whether racing a Formula 1 car on the streets of Monaco or a rally vehicle through treacherous mud baths in Kenya, and that's what makes motorsports so fascinating. The speed, strategy, skill, bravery, not to mention the sights and sounds, all combine to produce edge-of-your-seat drama. We capture all of that in this book.

Over the next hundred-plus pages we will guide you through some of the biggest sporting events in the world (and in the case of Monster Trucks we really do mean BIG!) and give you the facts and figures behind some true sporting legends, past and present. We'll explore some quirky traditions and enjoy the wackier motorsports, too. Yes, we're referring to lawn mower racing!

There's also a peek into the future, imagining what motorsport might look like in the next few years as technology continues to advance at lightning speed.

Who knows, it could be you starring in future editions of this book after helping a humanoid robot win the MotoGP title, or winning a Grand Prix in a shapeshifting car at speeds of 500km/h (310mph)*. It might not be as far-fetched as you think.

So, buckle up, motorsport fans! This fun, fact-filled book is about to take you on an unbelievable ride.

*Throughout the book, distances and speeds are given in metric or imperial depending on the system the competition officially uses. Conversions will usually follow in brackets.

FORMULA 1 RACING

Founded in 1950, the Formula 1 World Championship is the biggest motorsport competition on the planet. It stages 24 Grand Prix races in a season, across 21 countries and five continents, with a total audience of more than 1.5 billion.

WELCOME TO F1 RACING

The Formula 1 World Championship celebrated its 75th anniversary in 2025 and continues to wow fans around the world. Silverstone in England, which hosted the first Formula 1 Championship race in May 1950, welcomed nearly half a million fans to the 2024 British Grand Prix.

Silverstone is one of 24 races in the Formula 1 calendar, which visits five continents between March and December.

Taking centre stage are the 20 racing cars, which can reach speeds of up to 370km/h (230mph). The cars are so fast and sophisticated that multiple world champion Lewis Hamilton once said it felt like he was piloting a fighter jet.

GALLIC ROOTS

Grand Prix is French for 'grand prize'. The term was first used for a major motor race in 1906, when the Automobile Club de France launched a Grand Prix in Le Mans.

CLOSER THAN CLOSE

Teamwork and strategy are crucial in Formula 1 races, where every millisecond counts. Sometimes, even milliseconds can't separate drivers. In Canada, in 2024, drivers George Russell and Max Verstappen set identical times in qualifying. Russell took pole position, as his lap was recorded first, but Verstappen went on to win a thrilling race in wet conditions.

POSITION	TIME
1: George **RUSSELL** Mercedes	1:12.000
2: Max **VERSTAPPEN** Red Bull Racing	1:12.000
3: Lando **NORRIS** McLaren	1:12.021
4: Oscar **PIASTRI** McLaren	1:12.103

FULL HOUSE

An estimated crowd of 120,000 spectators attended the very first F1 Grand Prix race at Silverstone, England, in 1950, including the then reigning monarch King George VI.

1.80 SECONDS

The record-breaking time (in seconds) it took for the McLaren team to change all four tyres on Lando Norris' car during a pit stop at the 2023 Qatar Grand Prix.

11

A WORLD TOUR

Formula 1 racing is truly a global sport. The 2025 calendar features 24 rounds in 21 countries, across five continents. That's a lot of travelling, but the sport is mindful of its carbon footprint. This map shows the geographical flow of races, designed to limit distances between rounds.

Organisers have tried to create a better flow of races in certain regions to help reduce the travel distance between rounds. In 2024, they moved Japan to April, Azerbaijan to September, and scheduled Qatar with Abu Dhabi at the end of the year.

LESS IS MORE

The 2024 F1 race calendar saw teams travel about 123,000km (76,400mi) between races. This was 14,000km (8,600mi) fewer than the distance covered during the 2023 season.

	DATE	COUNTRY	LOCATION
1	March 14–16	**AUSTRALIA**	Melbourne
2	March 21–23	**CHINA**	Shanghai
3	April 4–6	**JAPAN**	Suzuka
4	April 11–13	**BAHRAIN**	Sakhir
5	April 18–20	**SAUDI ARABIA**	Jeddah
6	May 2–4	**USA**	Miami
7	May 16–18	**ITALY**	Imola
8	May 23–25	**MONACO**	Monaco
9	May 30–June 1	**SPAIN**	Barcelona
10	June 13–15	**CANADA**	Montreal
11	June 27–29	**AUSTRIA**	Spielberg
12	July 4–6	**UNITED KINGDOM**	Silverstone
13	July 25–27	**BELGIUM**	Spa
14	August 1–3	**HUNGARY**	Budapest
15	August 29–31	**NETHERLANDS**	Zandvoort
16	September 5–7	**ITALY**	Monza
17	September 19–21	**AZERBAIJAN**	Baku
18	October 3–5	**SINGAPORE**	Singapore
19	October 17–19	**USA**	Austin
20	October 24–26	**MEXICO**	Mexico City
21	November 7–9	**BRAZIL**	São Paulo
22	November 20–22	**USA**	Las Vegas
23	November 28–30	**QATAR**	Lusail
24	December 5–7	**ABU DHABI**	Yas Marina

RACE FOR POINTS

Points awarded at each race for a top ten finish:

1st = **25** pts.	6th = **8** pts.
2nd = **18** pts.	7th = **6** pts.
3rd = **15** pts.	8th = **4** pts.
4th = **12** pts.	9th = **2** pts.
5th = **10** pts.	10th= **1** pt.

There are extra points to win in the F1 sprint races, which were introduced in 2021. Currently, there are six sprint weekends in total during a season.

F1 SPRINT RACES

Held a day before the main race at six Grands Prix, the F1 Sprint sees drivers racing flat-out over 100km (62mi) – about one-third of the full Grand Prix distance – with no pit stops. The winner gets eight points.

The points are added up over the season, and sometimes it comes down to the final race to decide the winner. As well as the F1 Drivers' Championship, there are ten teams competing for the Constructors' Championship. Each team has two drivers, and their points are added together over the season.

LET'S GO RACING!

A race weekend lasts three days, building up to the Grand Prix itself on the Sunday. All circuits are unique, so the drivers need time to get themselves and their cars up to speed.

DAY 1: PRACTICE

The opening day begins with two 60-minute Free Practice sessions (FP1 and FP2), which are like warm-up sessions for the teams.

If it's a Sprint weekend, FP1 still takes place, followed by three short qualifying sessions for Saturday's 100-km (62mi) sprint race. This is an extra treat for the thousands of fans who attend each day. Points are awarded to the top eight finishers.

DID YOU KNOW?

In 1983, McLaren's British driver John Watson won the Grand Prix at Long Beach, USA, from 22nd on the grid. It is the lowest starting position for a race winner.

THE GRID POSITIONS

The grid positions are marked clearly on the circuit, alternating between left and right. The fastest two qualifiers start on the front row, and they have the advantage of a quick getaway, while those behind them try to navigate their way through heavy traffic.

19	17	15	13	11	9	7	5	3	1
20	18	16	14	12	10	8	6	4	2

DAY 2: QUALIFYING

Qualifying decides where each car will start on the grid for Sunday's main race.

Q1 and **Q2** determine positions 20-11 on the grid, with the slowest five cars eliminated at the end of each session.

Q3 then sorts out the top ten grid positions. The driver who sets the fastest lap time in Q3 secures pole.

DAY 3: RACE DAY

A race can last up to two hours, during which cars will complete anywhere between 44 and 78 laps of a track. Some tracks have more than 20 corners!

Before the race, there is the slow formation lap. The focus here is on warming the tyres and ensuring the car is in good working order, the equivalent of a long pre-race stretch. When all 20 cars are back in position on the starting grid, the fun begins. Five red lights turn on one by one before all go out at once, signalling the start of the race. Twenty cars dash to the first turn, with positions gained and lost in the opening few seconds.

WINNING FORMULA

A good race strategy is key to achieving a top-ten finish. Throughout the race, the driver keeps in radio contact with their team, who communicates the race plan. Fans on television can hear the conversations too, adding to the dramatic race coverage.

Mercedes Team Principal Toto Wolff instructs his driver during a race.

0.2 SECONDS

F1 drivers have extraordinary reaction times. On average, their cars pull away just 0.2 seconds after the starting lights go out.

TYRE OPTIONS

A race lasts between 75 minutes and two hours, and the winning margins are often tiny. Tyre changes are compulsory during a race, so deciding which tyres to use and when to use them can make all the difference. The tyres are colour-coded to make it easier to see which ones the drivers are using.

| Soft | Medium | Hard | Intermediate | Wet weather |

In dry conditions, cars use tyres without any grooves, known as slicks. Teams can choose to use soft, medium or hard slicks, but must use more than one type during a race.

Softs are the fastest, but also wear out the quickest, which could mean more pit stops. If it rains, the slicks are ditched for treaded intermediates or wets, offering better grip.

WHAT THE FLAGS MEAN

The black and white chequered flag is famously waved to signal the end of the race, but did you know there are several other coloured flags for drivers to be aware of? Here are what some others signal to a driver on the track.

 The track is clear (often waved after an incident).

 Danger ahead! Reduce speed, do not overtake.

 Let the car that is about to lap you overtake.

 Slippery surface ahead, slow down.

 The race is stopped. Proceed slowly to the pit lane.

 You are disqualified. Return to your pit garage.

F1 CARS

Since the 1950s, the Formula 1 car has developed from a relatively simple machine to the speedy, efficient, aerodynamic marvel on show today. Here are some of the highlights.

Formula 1 racing's first winning car was an **Alfa Romeo 158** in 1950. Despite its relatively heavy aluminium body, it could accelerate from 0 to 95km/h (60mph) in four seconds, and reach top speeds of around 306km/h (190mph).

The **Lotus 25**, which first appeared in the 1962 season, used a revolutionary monocoque chassis instead of the common tube-shaped frame. The car became known as the 'bathtub' because the driver's position in the cockpit made it seem like he was driving lying down.

1950s

1960s

Lotus 25

Alfa Romeo 158

The world's first carbon fibre racing car, the **McLaren MP4/1**, appeared in 1981. Carbon fibre technology made cars of the 1980s lighter and stronger.

1980s

1990s

Safety was increased in 1995 following the tragic deaths of Ayrton Senna and Roland Ratzenberger at Imola in 1994. To provide better head protection, the cockpit sides were raised, while planks were placed underneath the car to reduce downforce.

McLaren MP4/1

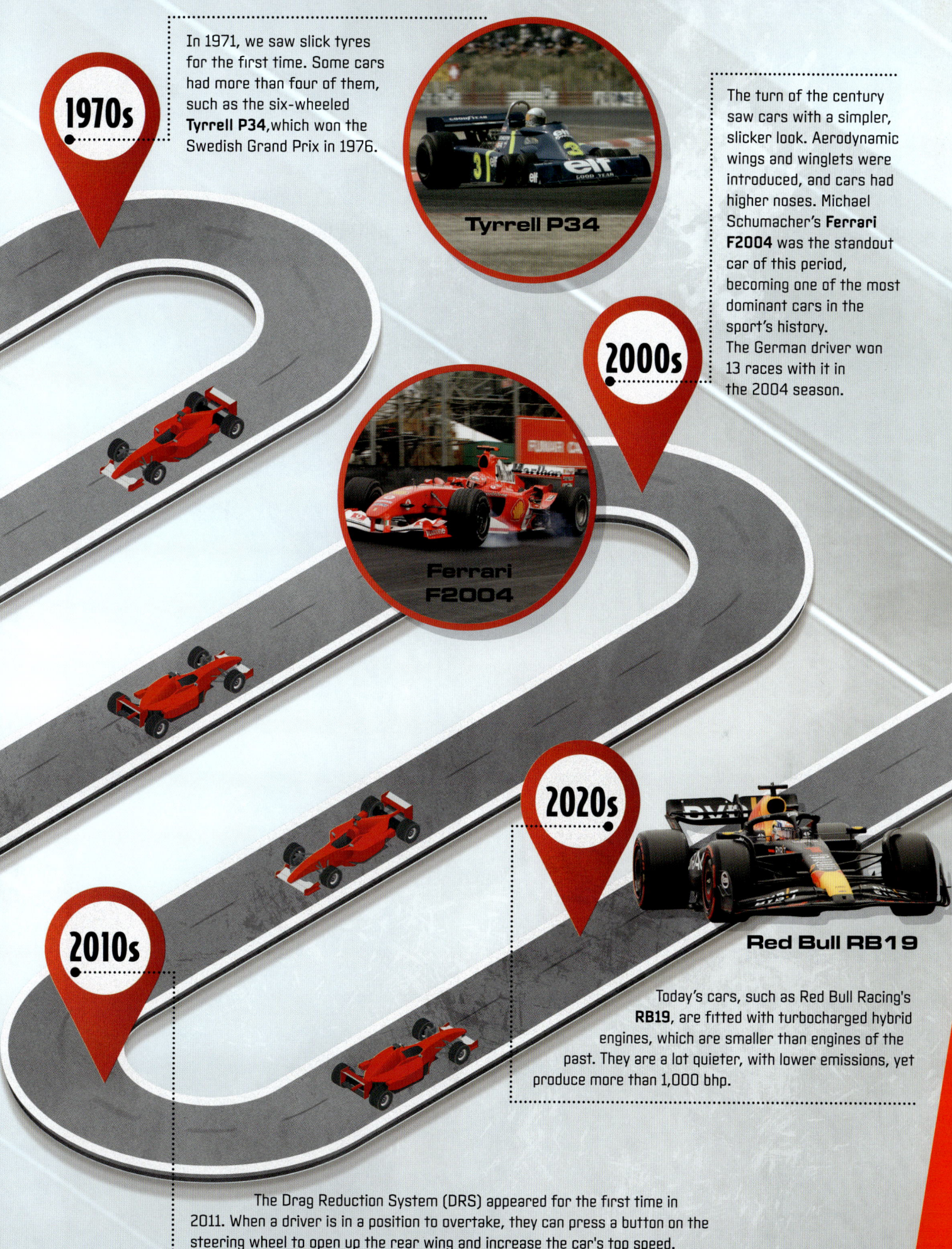

1970s

In 1971, we saw slick tyres for the first time. Some cars had more than four of them, such as the six-wheeled **Tyrrell P34**, which won the Swedish Grand Prix in 1976.

Tyrrell P34

The turn of the century saw cars with a simpler, slicker look. Aerodynamic wings and winglets were introduced, and cars had higher noses. Michael Schumacher's **Ferrari F2004** was the standout car of this period, becoming one of the most dominant cars in the sport's history. The German driver won 13 races with it in the 2004 season.

2000s

Ferrari F2004

2020s

Red Bull RB19

Today's cars, such as Red Bull Racing's **RB19**, are fitted with turbocharged hybrid engines, which are smaller than engines of the past. They are a lot quieter, with lower emissions, yet produce more than 1,000 bhp.

2010s

The Drag Reduction System (DRS) appeared for the first time in 2011. When a driver is in a position to overtake, they can press a button on the steering wheel to open up the rear wing and increase the car's top speed.

MEET THE TEAMS

Ten teams – each with two cars – line up at every Formula 1 race. Mercedes and Red Bull Racing have dominated the Constructors' Championship since 2010, but there are a lot of famous names on the grid. Here are the current contenders.

FERRARI

DEBUT: Monaco 1950

CONSTRUCTORS' TITLES: 16

RACE WINS: 248

PODIUMS: 830

BASE: Maranello, Italy

DRIVER TITLES: 15

FACT Ferrari is the only team to have competed in every Formula 1 season.

MERCEDES

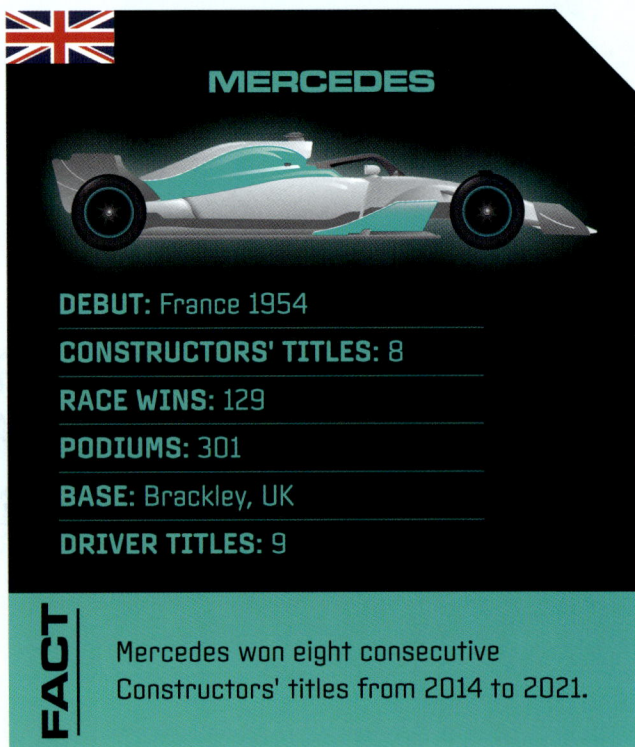

DEBUT: France 1954

CONSTRUCTORS' TITLES: 8

RACE WINS: 129

PODIUMS: 301

BASE: Brackley, UK

DRIVER TITLES: 9

FACT Mercedes won eight consecutive Constructors' titles from 2014 to 2021.

RED BULL RACING

DEBUT: Australia 2005

CONSTRUCTORS' TITLES: 6

RACE WINS: 123

PODIUMS: 285

BASE: Milton Keynes, UK

DRIVER TITLES: 8

FACT Red Bull Racing won 21 out of 22 races in 2023 – the most dominant season in Formula 1 racing's history.

WILLIAMS

DEBUT: Argentina 1978

CONSTRUCTORS' TITLES: 9

RACE WINS: 114

PODIUMS: 313

BASE: Grove, UK

DRIVER TITLES: 7

FACT Williams' first race victory (in 1979) and 100th race victory (in 1997) came at the British Grand Prix.

MCLAREN

DEBUT: Monaco 1966

CONSTRUCTORS' TITLES: 9

RACE WINS: 193

PODIUMS: 532

BASE: Woking, UK

DRIVER TITLES: 12

FACT

Lewis Hamilton won his first world title with McLaren in 2008.

ASTON MARTIN

DEBUT: Netherlands 1959

CONSTRUCTORS' TITLES: 0

RACE WINS: 0

PODIUMS: 9

BASE: Silverstone, UK

DRIVER TITLES: 0

FACT

Aston Martin returned in 2021 after a 61-year absence.

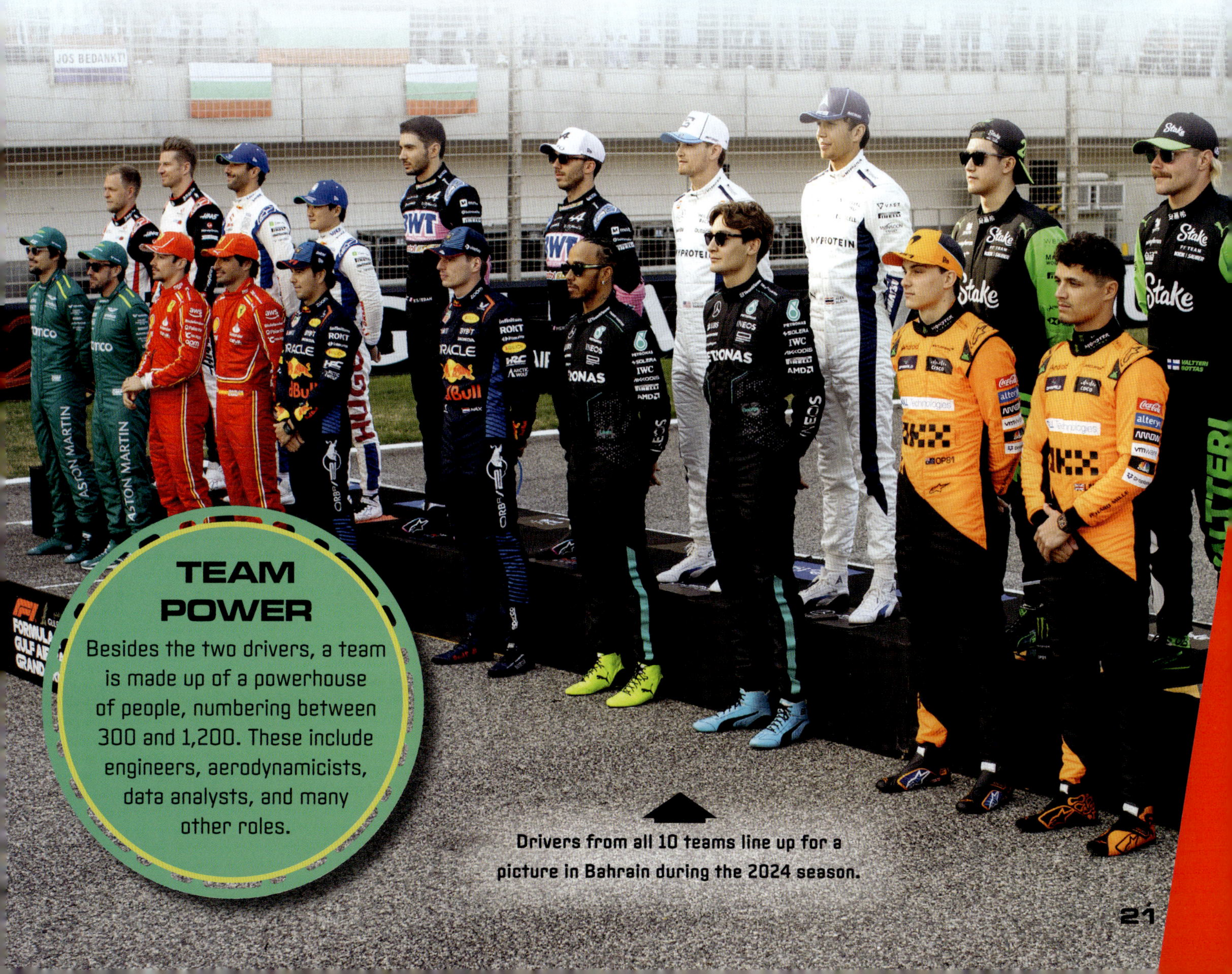

TEAM POWER

Besides the two drivers, a team is made up of a powerhouse of people, numbering between 300 and 1,200. These include engineers, aerodynamicists, data analysts, and many other roles.

▲ Drivers from all 10 teams line up for a picture in Bahrain during the 2024 season.

RACING BULLS

DEBUT: Bahrain 2006

CONSTRUCTORS' TITLES: 0

RACE WINS: 2

PODIUMS: 5

BASE: Faenza, Italy

DRIVER TITLES: 0

FACT
The team used to be Toro Rosso, then AlphaTauri, and lastly RB, before rebranding to Racing Bulls for 2025.

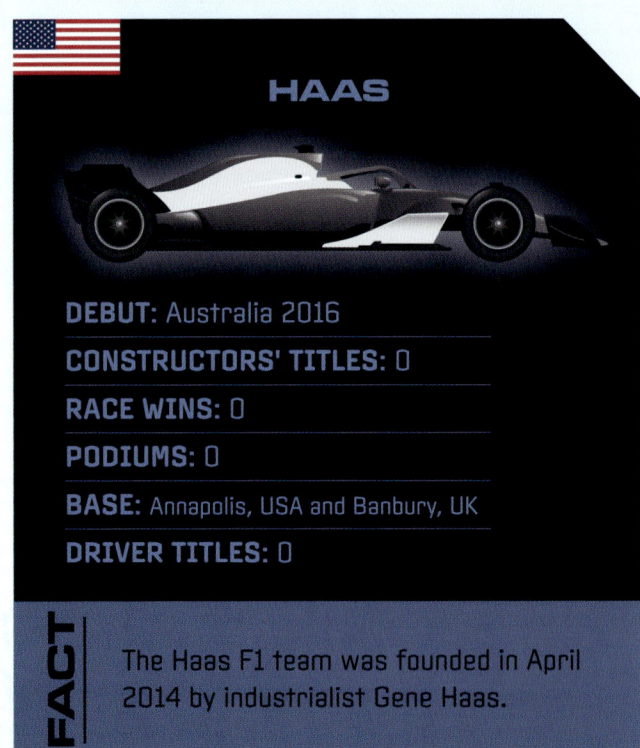

HAAS

DEBUT: Australia 2016

CONSTRUCTORS' TITLES: 0

RACE WINS: 0

PODIUMS: 0

BASE: Annapolis, USA and Banbury, UK

DRIVER TITLES: 0

FACT
The Haas F1 team was founded in April 2014 by industrialist Gene Haas.

BWT ALPINE

DEBUT: Bahrain 2021

CONSTRUCTORS' TITLES: 0

RACE WINS: 1

PODIUMS: 6

BASE: Enstone, UK

DRIVER TITLES: 0

FACT
Alpine was rebranded from Renault F1 Team for the 2021 season.

KICK SAUBER

DEBUT: South Africa 1993

CONSTRUCTORS' TITLES: 0

RACE WINS: 1

PODIUMS: 27

BASE: Hinwil, Switzerland

DRIVER TITLES: 0

FACT
In 2026, Kick Sauber will become the Audi Works Team.

INNOVATION

Behind every great team are brilliant, creative minds, finding ways to get the best possible performance out of their cars.

Engineer **Adrian Newey** was so influential in Red Bull Racing's recent success that Aston Martin offered him a salary of around £30m (US$39m) to join them in 2025. He knows how to make cars go faster!

AERODYNAMICS

Aerodynamics play an important role in quick lap times. The airflow around a racing car travelling at speed can create a downwards force, which pushes the tyres into the ground. This helps with grip, but it also creates drag, which slows the car down. The challenge is to get the balance right.

POWER SOURCE

Engines are called 'power units' in Formula 1 racing. They are hybrid, meaning they have more than one power source. By 2026, they will be nearly 50 per cent electric.

POWER

DOWNFORCE

GRIP

DRAG

This is why racing cars have front wings, to help direct the airflow outside the front tyre and to the underside of the car. They are like aircraft wings turned upside down, keeping the car grounded instead of taking off. Without them, cars would struggle to race around corners at high speed. To some outsiders, all F1 cars look the same. Take a closer look, and you'll notice a lot of subtle differences that make each one unique.

AT THE WHEEL

As well as elite skill, Formula 1 drivers require great physical and mental strength, piloting their cars at high speeds for up to two hours to win races and score points*.

FERNANDO ALONSO

The double F1 champion is a motorsport all-rounder. Alonso won the 2018–19 FIA World Endurance Championship. He has also raced in the IndyCar Series and the 2020 Dakar Rally.

NATIONALITY: Spain

TEAMS: Minardi (2001), Renault (2003–'06, 2008–'09), McLaren (2007, 2015–'18), Ferrari (2010–'14), Alpine (2021–'22), Aston Martin (2023–present)

DATE OF BIRTH: 29 July 1981

BIRTHPLACE: Oviedo, Spain

HEIGHT: 1.71m (5 ft 7 in)

STARTS	PODIUMS	WINS
406	106	32

POLE POSITIONS	WORLD CHAMPIONSHIPS	FASTEST LAPS
22	2	26

TOTAL POINTS 2,337

FACT A museum dedicated to Alonso opened in Spain in 2015, exhibiting more than 300 items from his racing career.

LEWIS HAMILTON

Lewis Hamilton holds the record for most wins (105), most pole positions (104), and shares the record for most Championship titles (7) with Michael Schumacher.

NATIONALITY: Great Britain

TEAMS: McLaren (2007–2012), Mercedes (2013–2024), Ferrari (2025–present)

DATE OF BIRTH: 07 January 1985

BIRTHPLACE: Stevenage, England

HEIGHT: 1.74m (5 ft 8 in)

STARTS	PODIUMS	WINS
361	202	105

POLE POSITIONS	WORLD CHAMPIONSHIPS	FASTEST LAPS
104	7	67

TOTAL POINTS 4,893.5

FACT Hamilton has the words 'Still I Rise' written on the back of his helmet and tattooed across his shoulders.

*Until 2010, no more than 10 points were awarded for a win.

CARLOS SAINZ

This exciting driver is getting better all the time and registered two wins in a season for the first time in 2024.

NATIONALITY: Spain

TEAMS: Toro Rosso (2015–'17), Renault (2017–'18), McLaren (2019–'20), Ferrari (2021–'24), Williams (2025–present)

DATE OF BIRTH: 01 September 1994

BIRTHPLACE: Madrid, Spain

HEIGHT: 1.78m (5 ft 10 in)

STARTS	PODIUMS	WINS
211	27	4

POLE POSITIONS	WORLD CHAMPIONSHIPS	FASTEST LAPS
6	0	4

TOTAL POINTS 1,277.5

FACT
His father, Carlos Sainz Sr., is a double World Rally champion.

MAX VERSTAPPEN

Max Verstappen has been making headlines since the age of 17 as F1's youngest-ever driver. A year later he became the youngest race winner at the 2016 Spanish Grand Prix.

NATIONALITY: Netherlands

TEAMS: Toro Rosso (2015–2016), Red Bull (2016–present)

DATE OF BIRTH: 30 September 1997

BIRTHPLACE: Hasselt, Belgium

HEIGHT: 1.81m (5 ft 11 in)

STARTS	PODIUMS	WINS
214	115	64

POLE POSITIONS	WORLD CHAMPIONSHIPS	FASTEST LAPS
42	4	33

TOTAL POINTS 3,110.5

FACT
Verstappen's dad, Jos, was an F1 racing driver who raced for eight seasons and achieved two podium places.

CHARLES LECLERC

The Ferrari driver is an exciting talent. In the 2024 season he won his home Monaco Grand Prix and Ferrari's home Grand Prix in Monza.

NATIONALITY: Monaco

TEAMS: Sauber (2018), Ferrari (2019–present)

DATE OF BIRTH: 16 October 1997

BIRTHPLACE: Monte Carlo, Monaco

HEIGHT: 1.80m (5 ft 11 in)

STARTS	PODIUMS	WINS
152	44	8

POLE POSITIONS	WORLD CHAMPIONSHIPS	FASTEST LAPS
26	0	10

TOTAL POINTS 1,477

FACT Leclerc was France's karting champion in 2009 at the age of 12.

GEORGE RUSSELL

Having partnered Lewis Hamilton for three seasons, he is now the senior driver at Mercedes, looking to make his mark in 2025.

NATIONALITY: Great Britain

TEAMS: Williams (2019-2021), Mercedes (2020 – one race, 2022–present)

DATE OF BIRTH: 15 February 1998

BIRTHPLACE: King's Lynn, England

HEIGHT: 1.85m (6 ft 1 in)

STARTS	PODIUMS	WINS
133	18	3

POLE POSITIONS	WORLD CHAMPIONSHIPS	FASTEST LAPS
5	0	8

TOTAL POINTS 787

FACT Russell was the first race winner to be disqualified in 30 years when his car was found to be underweight at the 2024 Belgian Grand Prix.

LANDO NORRIS

The McLaren driver was Max Verstappen's main challenger in 2024, recording four Grand Prix wins. His commanding victory in Singapore points to a very bright future.

NATIONALITY: Great Britain

TEAMS: McLaren (2019–present)

DATE OF BIRTH: 13 November 1999

BIRTHPLACE: Bristol, England

HEIGHT: 1.70m (5 ft 7 in)

STARTS	PODIUMS	WINS
133	30	5

POLE POSITIONS	WORLD CHAMPIONSHIPS	FASTEST LAPS
10	0	15

TOTAL POINTS 1,096

FACT Although Norris represents Great Britain, he is actually a dual citizen. His mother, Cisca, is from Belgium.

OSCAR PIASTRI

Lando Norris' team-mate at McLaren was born near the Australian Grand Prix venue in Melbourne and picked up his first points there as a Formula 1 racer in 2023.

NATIONALITY: Australia

TEAMS: McLaren (2023–present)

DATE OF BIRTH: 06 April 2001

BIRTHPLACE: Melbourne, Australia

HEIGHT: 1.78m (5 ft 10 in)

STARTS	PODIUMS	WINS
51	14	4

POLE POSITIONS	WORLD CHAMPIONSHIPS	FASTEST LAPS
2	0	4

TOTAL POINTS 488

FACT As a boy, Piastri raced remote-controlled cars and competed in Australia's national championships.

LEGENDS OF THE SPORT

Formula 1 racing has seen many motorsport legends emerge since its first championship in 1950. There have been 34 world champions, with Lewis Hamilton and Michael Schumacher topping the list as seven-time title winners. They are just two of many racing giants to have graced this sport.

GIUSEPPE FARINA

The winner of the first Formula 1 World Championship race at Silverstone in 1950, Farina went on to become the sport's first title winner.

NATIONALITY: Italy

ACTIVE YEARS: 1950-1955

BIRTHPLACE: Turin, Italy

HEIGHT: 1.78m (5ft 10in)

STARTS	PODIUMS	WINS
33	20	5

POLE POSITIONS	WORLD CHAMPIONSHIPS	FASTEST LAPS
5	1	5

CAREER POINTS 127.33

FACT Farina died in a car accident on his way to the 1966 French Grand Prix – a race he was just going to watch.

JUAN MANUEL FANGIO

Known as 'El Maestro', Fangio won five world titles with four different teams in the 1950s. In his 51 Grand Prix races he started from the front row 48 times.

NATIONALITY: Argentina

ACTIVE YEARS: 1950–'51, 1953–'58

BIRTHPLACE: Balcarce, Argentina

HEIGHT: 1.72m (5ft 8in)

STARTS	PODIUMS	WINS
51	35	24

POLE POSITIONS	WORLD CHAMPIONSHIPS	FASTEST LAPS
29	5	23

CAREER POINTS 277.64

FACT Fangio's five world titles were a long-standing record until Michael Schumacher surpassed him in 2003.

JIM CLARK

The double world champion also conquered the US by winning the 1965 Indianapolis 500. At the time of his tragic death in a crash in 1968, he had the most race wins in F1.

NATIONALITY: Great Britain

ACTIVE YEARS: 1960–1968

BIRTHPLACE: Kilmany in Fife, Scotland

HEIGHT: 1.71m (5ft 7in)

STARTS	PODIUMS	WINS
72	32	25

POLE POSITIONS	WORLD CHAMPIONSHIPS	FASTEST LAPS
33	2	28

CAREER POINTS 274

FACT While many F1 drivers come from racing backgrounds, Clark was born into a family of farmers from the Scottish borders.

NIKI LAUDA

A world champion with both Ferrari and McLaren, Lauda courageously returned to racing just six weeks after a life-threatening accident in the 1976 German Grand Prix.

NATIONALITY: Austria

ACTIVE YEARS: 1971–1985

BIRTHPLACE: Vienna, Austria

HEIGHT: 1.71m (5ft 7in)

STARTS	PODIUMS	WINS
171	54	25

POLE POSITIONS	WORLD CHAMPIONSHIPS	FASTEST LAPS
24	3	28

CAREER POINTS 420.5

FACT The accident Lauda suffered and his rivalry with James Hunt were reprised in the movie Rush in 2013.

29

ALAIN PROST

Alain Prost clinched his first title with McLaren in 1985. Nicknamed 'The Professor', for his intelligent approach to racing, Prost shared an intense rivalry with Ayrton Senna.

NATIONALITY: France

ACTIVE YEARS: 1980–1993

BIRTHPLACE: Lorette, France

HEIGHT: 1.65m (5ft 5in)

STARTS	PODIUMS	WINS
199	106	51

POLE POSITIONS	WORLD CHAMPIONSHIPS	FASTEST LAPS
33	4	41

CAREER POINTS 798.5

FACT Throughout his F1 career, Prost wore a simple crash helmet design featuring the colours of the French flag.

AYRTON SENNA

A three-time world champion with McLaren, his tragic death at the 1994 San Marino Grand Prix rocked the sport. For some, he is the greatest driver of all time.

NATIONALITY: Brazil

ACTIVE YEARS: 1984–1994

BIRTHPLACE: São Paulo, Brazil

HEIGHT: 1.76m (5ft 9in)

STARTS	PODIUMS	WINS
161	80	41

POLE POSITIONS	WORLD CHAMPIONSHIPS	FASTEST LAPS
65	3	19

CAREER POINTS 614

FACT Senna scored a record six wins at the Monaco Grand Prix between 1987 and 1993.

MICHAEL SCHUMACHER

The formidable German holds the record for most Championship titles (seven) alongside Lewis Hamilton, and won five in a row between 2000 and 2004.

NATIONALITY: Germany

ACTIVE YEARS: 1991–2006, 2010–2012

BIRTHPLACE: Hürth, Germany

HEIGHT: 1.74m (5ft 8.5in)

STARTS	PODIUMS	WINS
306	155	91

POLE POSITIONS	WORLD CHAMPIONSHIPS	FASTEST LAPS
68	7	77

CAREER POINTS 1,566

FACT

In 2007, Schumacher took the wheel of a slow taxi driver in Germany to get his family to the airport in time.

SEBASTIAN VETTEL

The youngest-ever world champion, Vettel won his first title at the age of 23 in 2010. By 26 he was a quadruple world champion, winning all four titles with Red Bull.

NATIONALITY: Germany

ACTIVE YEARS: 2006–2022

BIRTHPLACE: Heppenheim, Germany

HEIGHT: 1.75m (5ft 9in)

STARTS	PODIUMS	WINS
299	122	53

POLE POSITIONS	WORLD CHAMPIONSHIPS	FASTEST LAPS
57	4	38

CAREER POINTS 3,098

FACT

In the 2011 season, Vettel claimed 15 pole positions of 19 races, a record which still stands to this day.

THE CIRCUITS

There are 24 Grand Prix races in a season, each one held at a different venue. From the classic circuits of Silverstone, Monaco, and Suzuka, to the recent additions of Las Vegas, Miami, and Qatar, here are the highlights of the Formula 1 calendar.

MONACO

This famous street circuit in Monte Carlo has been part of the Formula 1 calendar since the very beginning. The narrow course presents few chances to overtake, but it's a favourite with fans and (most) drivers.

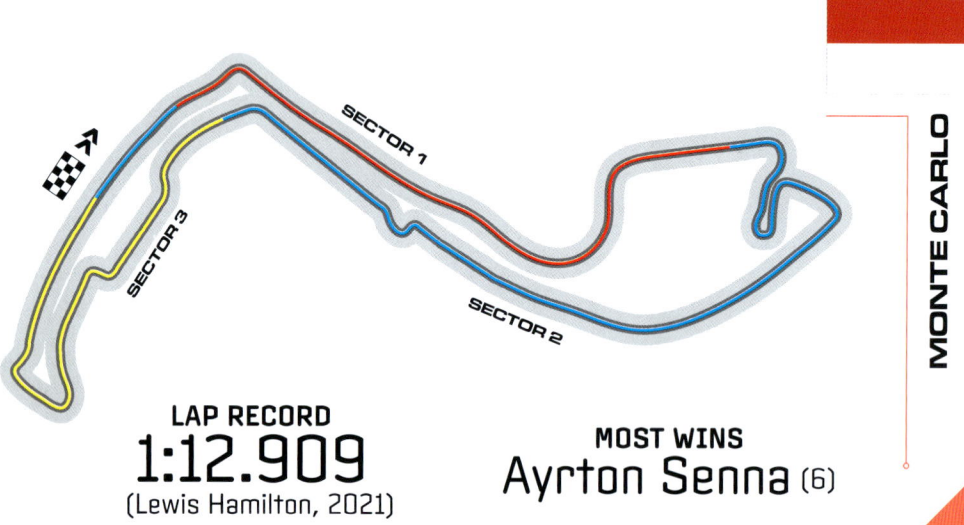

MONTE CARLO

LAP RECORD
1:12.909
(Lewis Hamilton, 2021)

MOST WINS
Ayrton Senna (6)

FIRST GRAND PRIX	CIRCUIT LENGTH	NUMBER OF LAPS	RACE DISTANCE
1950	3.337km	78	260.286km

SILVERSTONE

The home of the British Grand Prix, Silverstone held the first-ever Formula 1 championship race on May 13 1950. This former airfield is one of the fastest circuits and especially popular with Lewis Hamilton, who won here for a record ninth time in 2024.

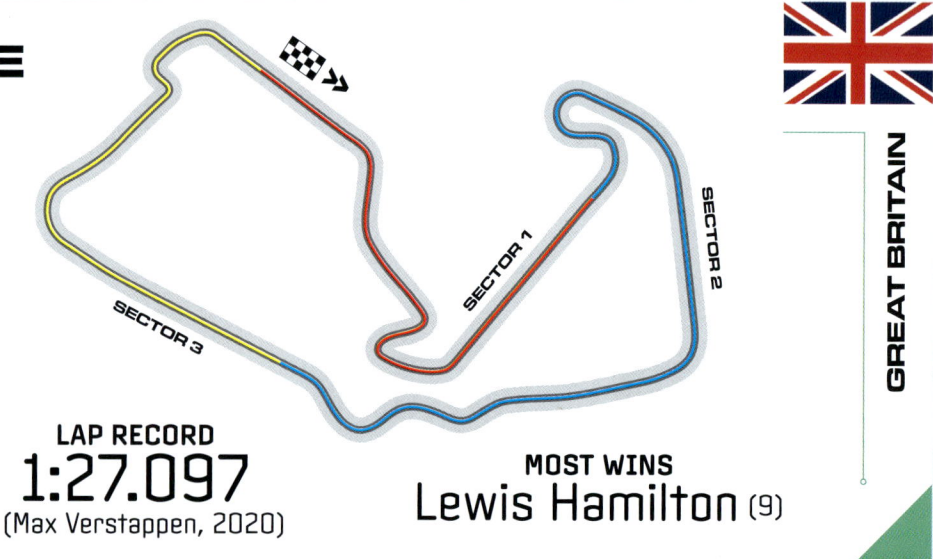

GREAT BRITAIN

LAP RECORD
1:27.097
(Max Verstappen, 2020)

MOST WINS
Lewis Hamilton (9)

FIRST GRAND PRIX	CIRCUIT LENGTH	NUMBER OF LAPS	RACE DISTANCE
1950	5.891km	52	306.198km

MELBOURNE

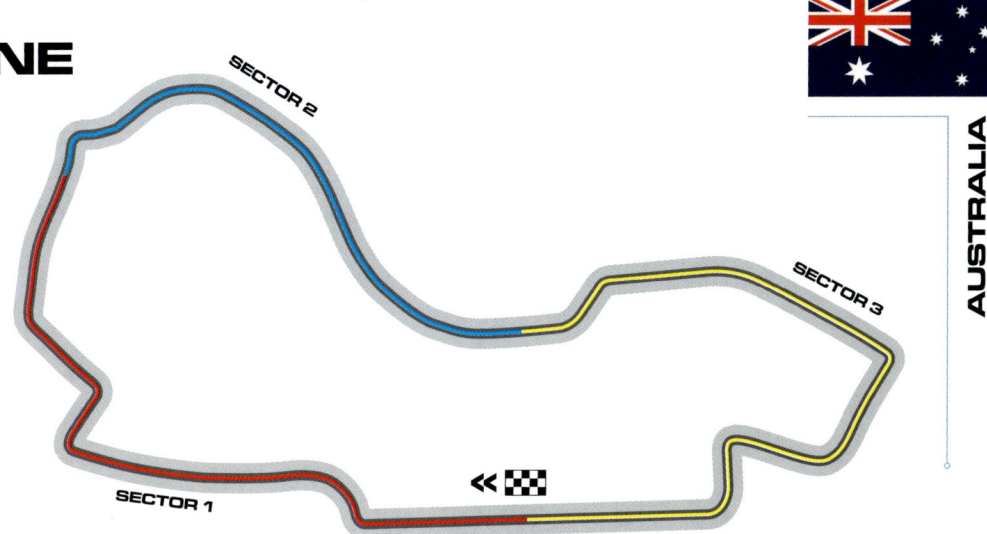

Set up around Melbourne's Albert Park Lake, this street circuit often hosts the season's opening race of. It was modified in 2021 to make racing even faster, and attracts crowds of more than 130,000 on race day.

SECTOR 2

SECTOR 3

SECTOR 1

AUSTRALIA

LAP RECORD
1:19.813
(Charles Leclerc, 2024)

MOST WINS
Michael Schumacher (4)

FIRST GRAND PRIX	CIRCUIT LENGTH	NUMBER OF LAPS	RACE DISTANCE
1996	**5.278km**	**58**	**306.124km**

SUZUKA

The only one of the 24 circuits to have a 'figure of eight' layout, with a long back straight crossing over the front section via an overpass. It's fast and challenging, and loved by drivers.

SECTOR 2

SECTOR 3

SECTOR 1

JAPAN

LAP RECORD
1:30.965
(Andrea Kimi Antonelli, 2019)

MOST WINS
Michael Schumacher (6)

FIRST GRAND PRIX	CIRCUIT LENGTH	NUMBER OF LAPS	RACE DISTANCE
1987	**5.807km**	**53**	**307.471km**

AUSTIN

The Circuit of the Americas (COTA) outside Austin, Texas, was designed with other famous tracks in mind. There are nods to Silverstone, Hockenheim, and Istanbul, but its most striking feature is the hairpin (a tight, U-shaped bend) just after the start.

SWIFT CIRCUIT: In 2016, popstar Taylor Swift performed here as part of the race weekend, helping promote the sport to a new set of fans.

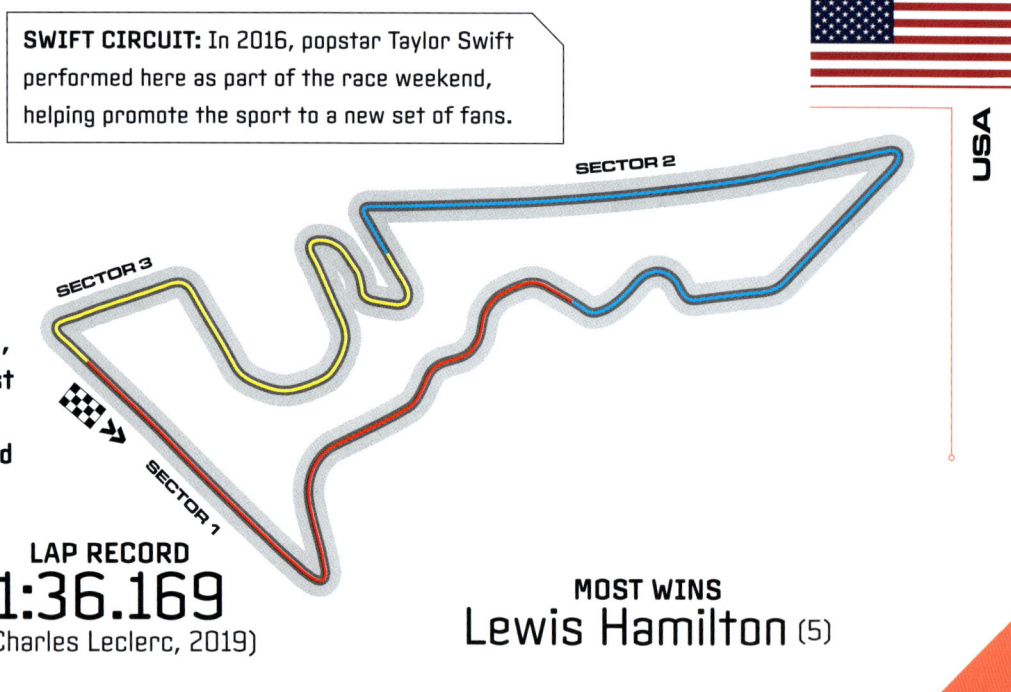

USA

LAP RECORD
1:36.169
(Charles Leclerc, 2019)

MOST WINS
Lewis Hamilton (5)

FIRST GRAND PRIX	CIRCUIT LENGTH	NUMBER OF LAPS	RACE DISTANCE
2012	5.513km	56	308.405km

SINGAPORE

Singapore's Marina Bay Street Circuit held the first night race in 2008, and it continues to stage races under the lights. Even at night, the humidity makes it one of the most physically demanding tests for drivers.

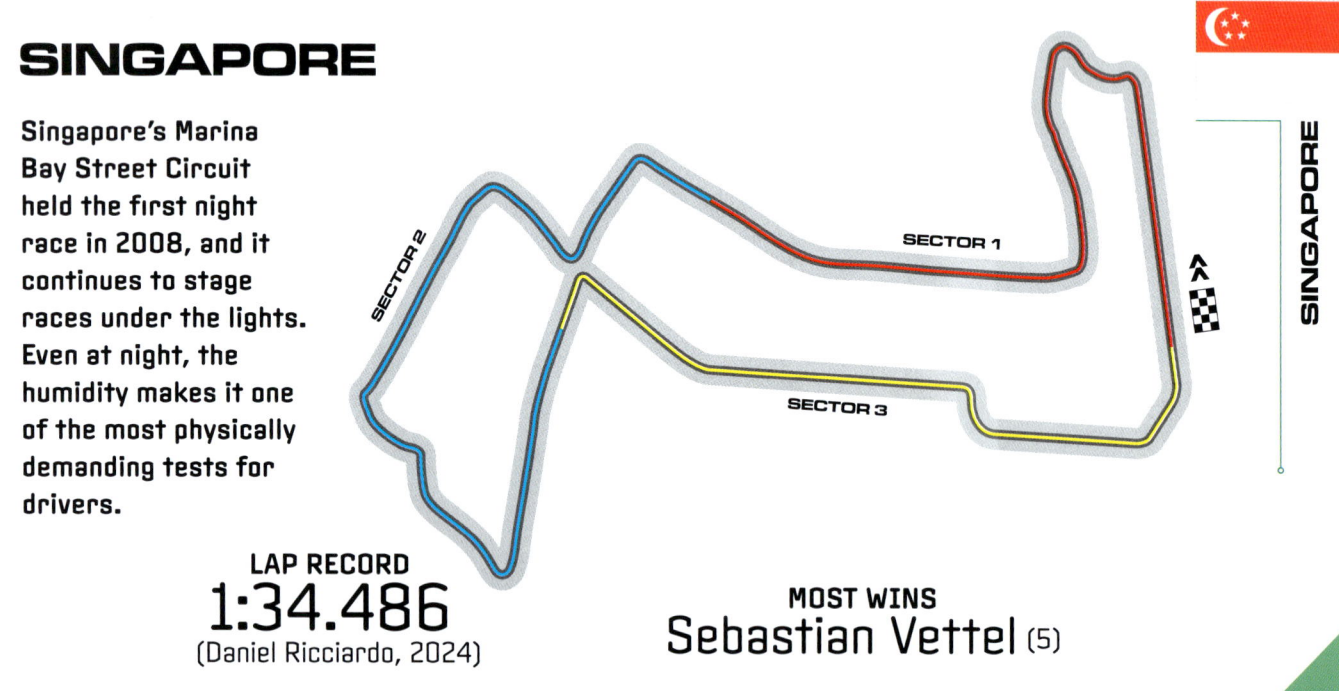

SINGAPORE

LAP RECORD
1:34.486
(Daniel Ricciardo, 2024)

MOST WINS
Sebastian Vettel (5)

FIRST GRAND PRIX	CIRCUIT LENGTH	NUMBER OF LAPS	RACE DISTANCE
2008	4.94km	62	306.143km

MONZA

This legendary Italian track is more than a century old, having hosted its first race in 1922. Its long straights make it one of the fastest circuits, enabling cars to travel at full throttle for 80 per cent of the lap.

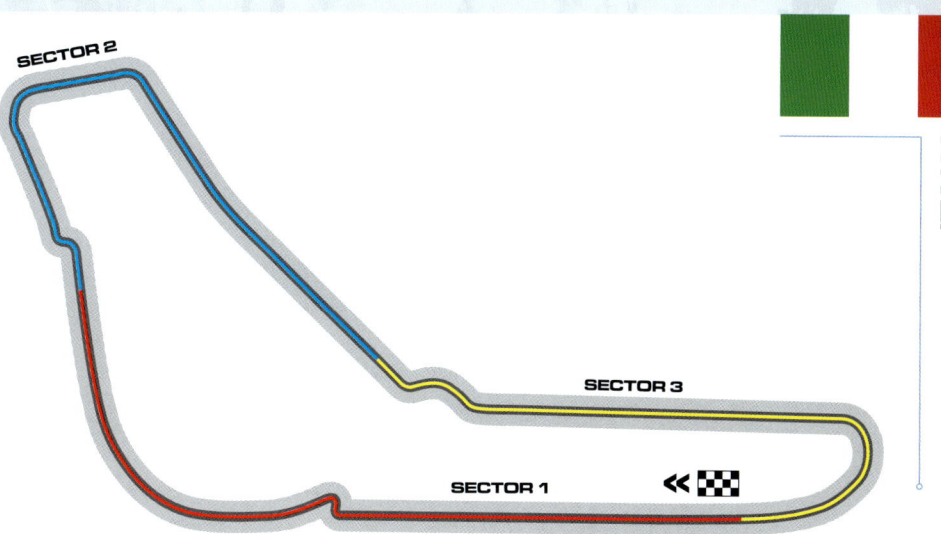

LAP RECORD
1:21.046
(Rubens Barrichello, 2004)

MOST WINS
Michael Schumacher (5)
Lewis Hamilton (5)

FIRST GRAND PRIX	CIRCUIT LENGTH	NUMBER OF LAPS	RACE DISTANCE
1950	**5.793km**	**53**	**306.72km**

MONTREAL

The Circuit Gilles-Villeneuve is named after the great Canadian racer who won here with Ferrari in 1978. Drivers should beware of the 'Wall of Champions', so-called because it has been hit by a surprising number of champions over the years.

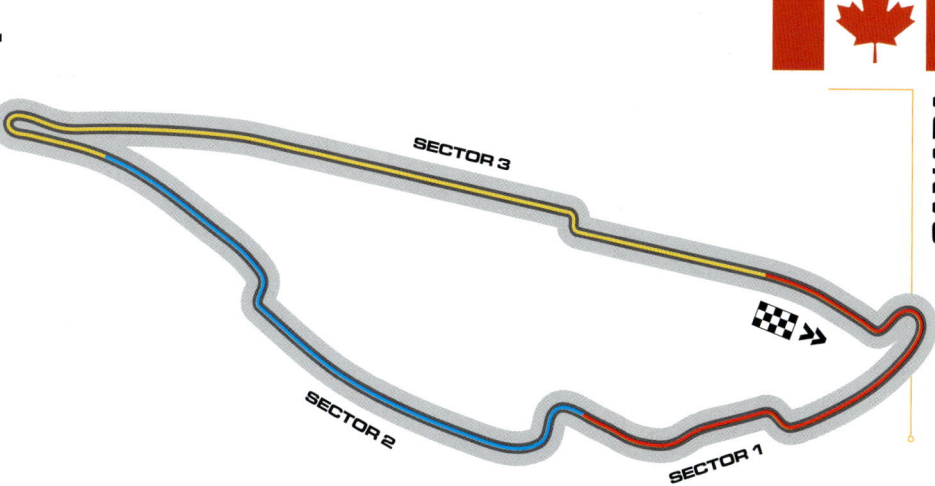

LAP RECORD
1:13.078
(Valtteri Bottas, 2019)

MOST WINS
Michael Schumacher (7)
Lewis Hamilton (7)

FIRST GRAND PRIX	CIRCUIT LENGTH	NUMBER OF LAPS	RACE DISTANCE
1978	**4.361km**	**70**	**305.27km**

ROUTES TO THE TOP

How do you become a Formula 1 champion? Lewis Hamilton, Max Verstappen, Ayrton Senna, and many other greats began in karting – and there's a clear path to the top if you have the skill, determination, and a bit of luck.

Max Verstappen took part in his first kart race when he was seven, as did Lando Norris. Lewis Hamilton was eight. Karting offers a perfect introduction to motorsports, teaching vital racing skills such as overtaking, track positioning, and race strategy.

The karts themselves are very low to the ground, making everything feel twice as fast and exhilarating. A racing kart in the cadet class (eight to 12 years) travels at speeds of between 50 and 80km/h (30 and 50mph).

◄ Max Verstappen in action during his karting days.

FORMULA 4

Launched in 2013, Formula 4 is the next step up from karting.

This racing category is intended for junior drivers and gives them the chance to handle more powerful vehicles on larger tracks. F4 cars can reach speeds of up to 250km/h (155mph).

F4 features several national championships. In 2024, 21-year-old Abbi Pulling (left) became the first female driver to win a British F4 race at Brands Hatch.

ENGINE SIZE

1.6L
4-CYLINDER

FORMULA 3

The Formula 3 Championship visits nine countries over ten rounds as part of the Formula 1 race weekend.

This gives aspiring young drivers a chance to shine in front of F1 teams at famous circuits such as Melbourne, Silverstone, and Monza.

Racing on these F1 tracks helps them to hone their skills both in speed and in tyre management, and prepares them to move up the motorsport ladder.

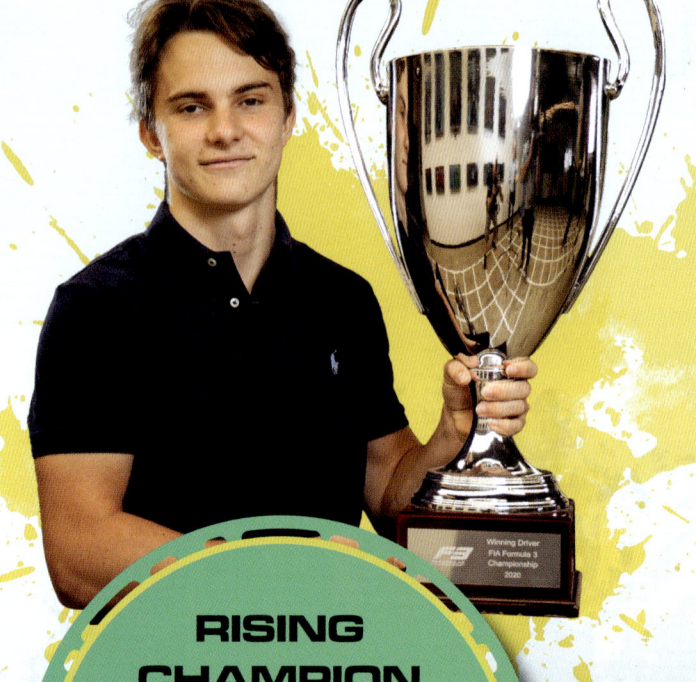

RISING CHAMPION

Australian driver Oscar Piastri – now driving for McLaren in Formula 1 – was Formula 3 champion in 2020 and Formula 2 champion the following year.

FRIDAY	SATURDAY	SUNDAY
Free Practice 45 mins	**Sprint Race** 40 mins + 1 lap	**Feature Race*** 45 mins + 1 lap
Qualifying 30 mins		No compulsory pit stops

*Before the F1 Grand Prix

ENGINE SIZE

3.4L
6-CYLINDER

BACK TO FRONT

The starting grid for the Sprint Race is reversed for the top 12 finishers of Friday's qualifying session, so the fastest qualifier starts the race in 12th place.

FORMULA 2

Formula 2 – like Formula 3 – shares several race weekends with Formula 1.

It features young drivers within touching distance of the top level. In recent years, Charles Leclerc, George Russell, Lando Norris, and Gabriel Bortoleto have all graduated successfully from F2 to F1.

Formula 2 cars are designed to be as close to F1 cars as possible, providing the perfect training ground for those making the step up. All cars are the same, which makes each race a true test of driving skill.

HIGH HOPES

After excelling in Formula 2, Brazilian racer Enzo Fittipaldi hopes to follow in the footsteps of his grandad, Emerson, by competing and winning in F1 racing.

FRIDAY	SATURDAY	SUNDAY
Free Practice 45 mins	**Sprint Race*** 120km or 45 mins + 1 lap	**Feature Race** 45 mins + 1 lap
Qualifying 30 mins		**Grand Prix** 170km or 60 mins + 1 lap

*The starting grid is reversed for the top ten qualifiers, so the fastest starts in 10th. This gives the best drivers a chance to showcase their overtaking skills.

F1 ACADEMY

Set up in 2023, the F1 Academy has been created for young female drivers, with the aim of making motorsports more diverse and accessible. Only two female drivers have ever started a Formula 1 race, but this initiative could soon change that.

ENGINE SIZE
3.4L
V6 TURBO

FORMULA E

Formula E is a racing championship for the world's fastest electric vehicles. The cars can reach a top speed of 320km/h (200mph). That's some serious battery power!

Formula E began when the championship's founder, Alejandro Agag, met FIA President Jean Todt in a Paris restaurant and scribbled the idea on the back of a napkin! Launched in 2014, this predominantly street racing series has grown rapidly and now features 16 rounds in 10 countries. The season usually starts at the end of the year and runs until the European summer, finishing in London, UK, in July.

Like in Formula 1, there are separate championships for drivers and teams. Twenty-two drivers and 11 race teams compete in the series. Points are awarded to the top ten finishers, with 25 points going to the winner and an extra point for the driver with the fastest lap. There are also three points for securing pole position at the front of the grid.

RACE FORMAT

Most events take place over a single day, with a practice session followed by qualifying and then the race itself.

Qualifying is set up a bit like a football tournament, starting with a group stage and ending in a two-car face-off, known as The Final Duel.

QUALIFYING

A group stage session lasts ten minutes, with the fastest four from each group progressing to the duels knockout stage, where drivers go head-to-head over one flying lap. The winner of the final duel takes pole position. It's a deliberately unpredictable format, providing entertainment for the fans.

Races have a set number of laps and usually last under an hour. However, one rain-affected race in London at the end of Season 9 turned into a two-hour-13-minute epic!

SPECIALIST RACERS

Formula E is so specialised that drivers must hold a valid e-driving licence before they can race.

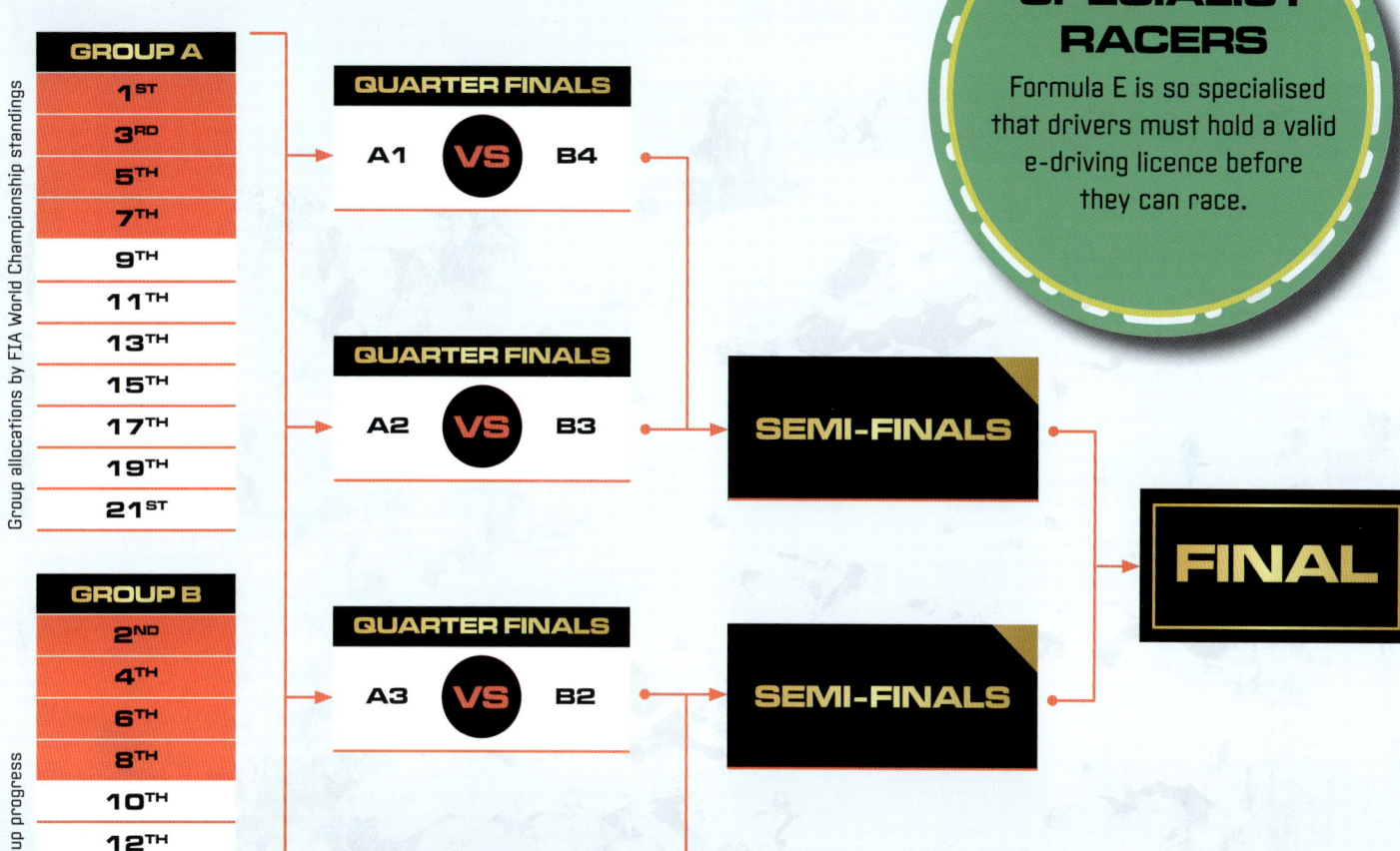

Group allocations by FIA World Championship standings

GROUP A
- 1ST
- 3RD
- 5TH
- 7TH
- 9TH
- 11TH
- 13TH
- 15TH
- 17TH
- 19TH
- 21ST

Fastest four from each group progress

GROUP B
- 2ND
- 4TH
- 6TH
- 8TH
- 10TH
- 12TH
- 14TH
- 16TH
- 18TH
- 20TH
- 22ND

QUARTER FINALS A1 VS B4
QUARTER FINALS A2 VS B3
QUARTER FINALS A3 VS B2
QUARTER FINALS A4 VS B1

SEMI-FINALS
SEMI-FINALS

FINAL

ATTACK MODE

POWER ZONE

Each circuit has a special Activation Zone, which gives drivers extra power. To use this the driver must leave the racing line and drive through a marked area.* It's a risk – but often a risk worth taking.

WATCH OUT!

When a car goes into attack mode, the LED lights on the halo above the cockpit turn electric blue.

PUSH THE BUTTON

All drivers must use Attack Mode for a total of eight minutes in a race. The mode is activated by a button on the steering wheel. Deciding when to do it is key to success!

*Pit Boost: New for 2025, cars will be able to make a pit stop for a 30-second battery recharge.

FORMULA E

TOP TEAMS

Motorsport is a team game and Formula E has some famous names competing for the World Teams' Championship. Jaguar took their first title in 2024, with New Zealand's Mitch Evans and Nick Cassidy as the team's drivers. Below is a list of the most successful teams.

TEAM	RACES	WINS	PODIUMS
NISSAN	136	21	50
ENVISION	136	16	53
JAGUAR TCS	115	17	47
LOLA YAMAHA ABT	119	14	47
TAG HEUER PORSCHE	78	12	25
ANDRETTI	136	11	37

FAST FAMILY

Formula E's first champion was the son of a three-time Formula 1 world champion, Nelson Piquet. Brazil's Nelson Piquet Jr. won the inaugural Formula E title in 2015.

ELECTRIC SUPER CAR

Formula E is now into its second decade and its engineering is evolving at quite a pace. Cutting-edge technology is helping the cars go faster and further every season. The latest vehicles have a 30 per cent faster acceleration than anything racing in F1.

What's more, the Formula E cars are more sustainable, with 40 per cent of the energy used being recaptured and used again. Check out some of the impressive stats behind the GEN3 EVO model (right).

GEN3 EVO

Max Power: 350kW (470bhp)

Max Regeneration: 600kW

Energy Recovery: Over 40 per cent

Top Speed: 320km/h (200mph)

The GEN3 EVO race car was unveiled in April 2024, ahead of the Monaco E-Prix.

RAPID PICKUP

Did you know the GEN3 EVO race car can accelerate from 0-100km/h in 1.86 seconds, or 0-60mph in just 1.82 seconds?! It is also the world's first net zero carbon racing car.

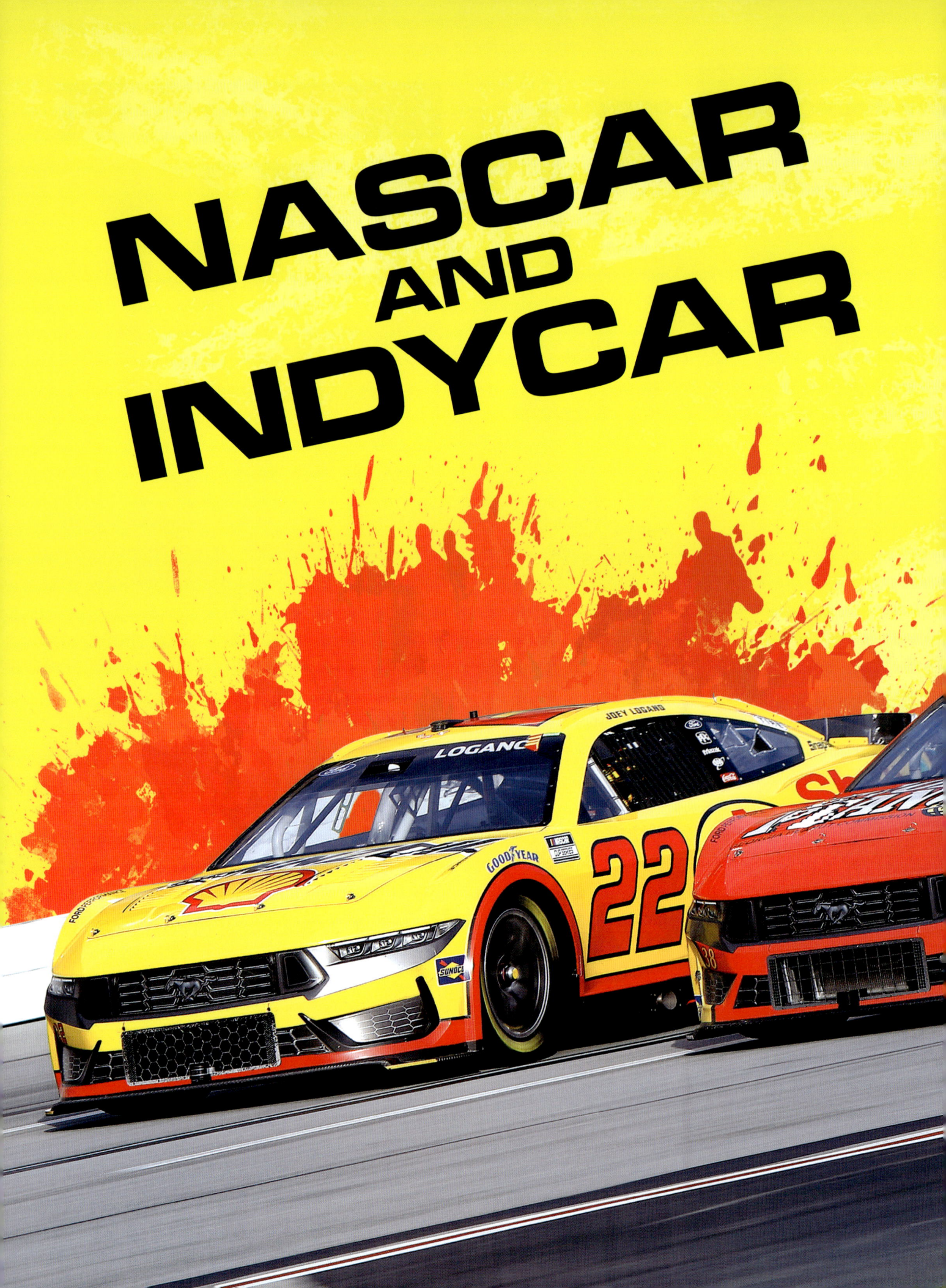

NASCAR AND INDYCAR

Based in the USA, these two famous series are home to the prestigious Daytona 500 and Indianapolis 500 races. While the car speeds are similar to those in Formula 1, the circuits – many of which are oval – are very different.

RACE FOR AMERICA

NASCAR is among the largest spectator sports in the USA. It features stock cars racing for hundreds of miles at great speeds, many on oval racetracks with banked turns, and it starts every year with the 'Great American Race', the **Daytona 500**.

There are 26 races in the regular season, followed by a 10-race play-off, which ends with a winner-takes-all championship race held with a full grid, but just four drivers in contention for the title.

That's a lot of racing. In fact, the combined distance covered by all drivers is around 725,000km (450,500mi), which would almost get you to the moon and back. NASCAR really is out of this world!

DREAM BIG

NASCAR's story began in December 1947, when Bill France founded the National Association for Stock Car Auto Racing (NASCAR). 'Big Bill', – as he was known – was a mechanic with a love for stock car racing, and he organised the very first NASCAR race at Daytona Beach, won by Red Byron (right) in a Ford, in February 1948.

The first full season in 1949 featured just eight races. The opener – at Charlotte Speedway – was won by Jim Roper, who decided to enter after reading about it in his local paper.

Contrast that with NASCAR's 75th anniversary season in 2023, when an estimated 2.5 million fans flocked to see live racing!

0.001 SECONDS

Kyle Larson (see p.53) recorded the smallest winning margin in NASCAR's history when he beat Chris Buescher by inches at Kansas Speedway in 2024.

212.809

The record speed in mph (342.483km/h) for a NASCAR race car, set by Bill Elliott in a Ford Thunderbird at Talladega Superspeedway in 1987.

STAGES OF A RACE

NASCAR has three stages to each race (four at NASCAR's longest race, the Coca-Cola 600). Introduced in 2017, this format offers bonus points for the top ten finishers in Stages 1 and 2, keeping excitement levels high throughout the race.

The final stage determines the race's overall winner and, as so often in motorsports, strategy plays a big part. With points on offer at three different stages of the race, knowing when to pit can be key.

| Race win | = | **40** pts. |
| Stage win | = | **10** pts. |

BUMP AND RUN

Cars are fitted with bumpers and can cope with minor contact. It's common for NASCAR racers to nudge each other during a race, either to help a team-mate or slip past a rival!

THE TRACKS

Although most NASCAR tracks are oval-shaped, several road courses are featured in the schedule, too. Whatever their shape, all are unique. Here are some of the sport's best-known venues in the USA.

TALLADEGA
SUPERSPEEDWAY

NASCAR's biggest, steepest, and fastest track. Bill Elliott's speed record (see p.47) was set here in 1987.

LOCATION: TALLADEGA, ALABAMA

LENGTH: 2.66MI (4.28KM)

TURNS: 4

FIRST RACE: 1969

CROWD CAPACITY: 80,000

DAYTONA
INTERNATIONAL SPEEDWAY

Built to replace the beach-road course of NASCAR's early days, this track hosts one of the sport's famous races, the Daytona 500.

LOCATION: DAYTONA BEACH, FLORIDA

LENGTH: 2.5MI (4.02KM)

TURNS: 4

FIRST RACE: 1959

CROWD CAPACITY: 123,500

BRISTOL MOTOR
SPEEDWAY

Also called Thunder Valley, this short oval track is famous for its night races, which first appeared on the NASCAR billing in 1978.

LOCATION: BRISTOL, TENNESSEE

LENGTH: 0.533MI (0.858KM)

TURNS: 4

FIRST RACE: 1961

CROWD CAPACITY: 146,000

MARTINSVILLE
SPEEDWAY

The shortest and oldest track in NASCAR, this has hosted NASCAR Cup Series races every year since 1949.

LOCATION: RIDGEWAY, VIRGINIA

LENGTH: 0.526MI (0.856KM)

TURNS: 4

FIRST RACE: 1949

CROWD CAPACITY: 65,000

RICHMOND
RACEWAY

Something of a short-track gem, this is the only course with a 1.21km (0.75mi) layout. An infield fanzone adds to its appeal.

LOCATION: RICHMOND, VIRGINIA

LENGTH: 0.75 MI (1.21KM)

TURNS: 4

FIRST RACE: 1953

CROWD CAPACITY: 51,000

CHARLOTTE MOTOR
SPEEDWAY

Home of NASCAR's longest race, the Coca-Cola 600, which is a unique day/night race that finishes under the lights.

LOCATION: CONCORD, NORTH CAROLINA

LENGTH: 1.5MI (2.41KM)

TURNS: 4

FIRST RACE: 1960

CROWD CAPACITY: 95,000

WATKINS GLEN
INTERNATIONAL

One of seven road courses in NASCAR's schedule, 'The Glen' also hosted the F1 USA Grand Prix from 1961 to 1980.

LOCATION: WATKINS GLEN, NEW YORK

LENGTH: 2.45MI (3.94KM)

TURNS: 8

FIRST RACE: 1986

CROWD CAPACITY: 38,900*

MICHIGAN
INTERNATIONAL SPEEDWAY

This fast, wide track has seen many famous finishes, with NASCAR Hall of Famer Cale Yarborough taking the very first win in 1969.

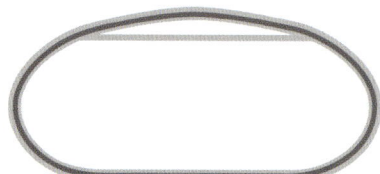

LOCATION: BROOKLYN, MICHIGAN

LENGTH: 2.0MI (3.22KM)

TURNS: 4

FIRST RACE: 1969

CROWD CAPACITY: 56,000

*The overall capacity can exceed 100,000 with extra temporary seating and infield zones

RACE CARS

NASCAR is stock car racing, but the definition of a stock car has changed over the years. In the sport's early days, the cars came straight from the production line. They were regular street vehicles and even had normal doors. Drivers didn't need to climb through the windows back then!

In the 1960s, a new generation of NASCAR cars arrived. Teams were allowed to adjust the chassis to cope with new superspeedways, which are tracks more than two miles long (3.22km), while doors were ditched for safety reasons.

Fibreglass bodies arrived in the 1990s, and in 2007 the Car of Tomorrow was launched, with much improved safety and a flashy rear wing.

Modern day stock cars look more like showroom models, plus they have lots of cool upgrades. The Next Gen car, which first appeared in the 2022 season, has an in-car camera and can transmit real-time data to its team and fans. Although it looks very different from the cars used in Formula 1 and Indycar racing, the car's design is just as aerodynamic to ensure top speed. At the same time, NASCAR is developing the technology to achieve net zero carbon emissions by 2035.

ENGINE
Delivers a maximum output of 670bhp (500kW) at most racetracks.

MIGHTY GRIP
NASCAR cars can generate enough downforce to drive upside down! At high speeds, the air flowing over the car's body creates a downward force that helps to keep the car stuck to the track.

BUMPERS
Car fitted with front and rear bumpers for increased safety.

BODY
Designed to manipulate airflow to achieve the best balance, speed, and control.

ROLL CAGE
Designed to withstand serious impacts and protect the driver in the cabin.

SPOILER
Helps the car stay on the track and increases traction at high speeds.

DIFFUSER
Speeds up airflow under the car, increasing downforce while reducing drag.

BRAKES
Designed to perform under the most severe and demanding racing conditions.

LUCKY NUMBER
One of the most important features of the car, to fans anyway, is the car number. Did you know that the most successful number in NASCAR's history is 11? The no. 11 has had 236 wins over the years, including 55 for three-time NASCAR champion Cale Yarborough.

TYRES
Larger 46cm (18in.) in diameter – ideal for short tracks and road courses.

HOW THE SEASON WORKS

The regular season is made up of 26 races, starting each year with the famous Daytona 500. At the end of the regular season, a regular-season champion is crowned.

At each race, 40 points are awarded to the winner, plus a further maximum 20 points are on offer over the two stages. So that's a potential 60 points if a driver has the perfect Sunday (or 70 points in NASCAR's longest race, the Coca-Cola 600, which has three stages).

GRID PLACING

Up to 40 cars may take part in any given Cup Series race. After the first round of 40, the top 10 fastest cars go up against each other in the second round to determine the order in which they will start the race. The remaining drivers are assigned a spot based on their first-round qualifying lap.

PLAYOFFS TO VICTORY

At the end of the regular season, 16 drivers advance to the playoffs and points totals are reset. Three elimination rounds take place – each consisting of three races – before we reach the NASCAR Cup Series Championship Race, where the remaining four drivers compete for the title. NASCAR's playoff system ensures excitement right to the very end of the season.

ROUND OF 16

ROUND OF 12

ROUND OF 8

QUARTER FINALS

FINAL

NASCAR ALL-STAR RACE
NORTH WILKESBORO 2024

PAY TO THE ORDER OF **Joey Logano**

ONE MILLION AND **00 / 100**

MAY 19,

$ 1,000

DOLLARS

BUSCH LIGHT   Coca-Cola   GEICO   xfi

KING KYLE

Kyle Larson (left) is a living legend in NASCAR racing. Now driving for Hendrick Motorsports, he has 31 race victories to his name and has qualified for the NASCAR Playoffs in 2016–'19 and 2021–'24.

THE RACE FOR A MILLION

Midway through the season, drivers compete in the All-Star Race, an exhibition race for stars past and present. There are no championship points at stake, but there is a US$1m cheque for the winning team.

DAYTONA 500

Every February, the NASCAR season starts with the world-famous Daytona 500 race. Held at the Daytona International Speedway in Daytona Beach, Florida, USA, it is one of the most-watched motorsport events in the world.

71
WeatherTech
19

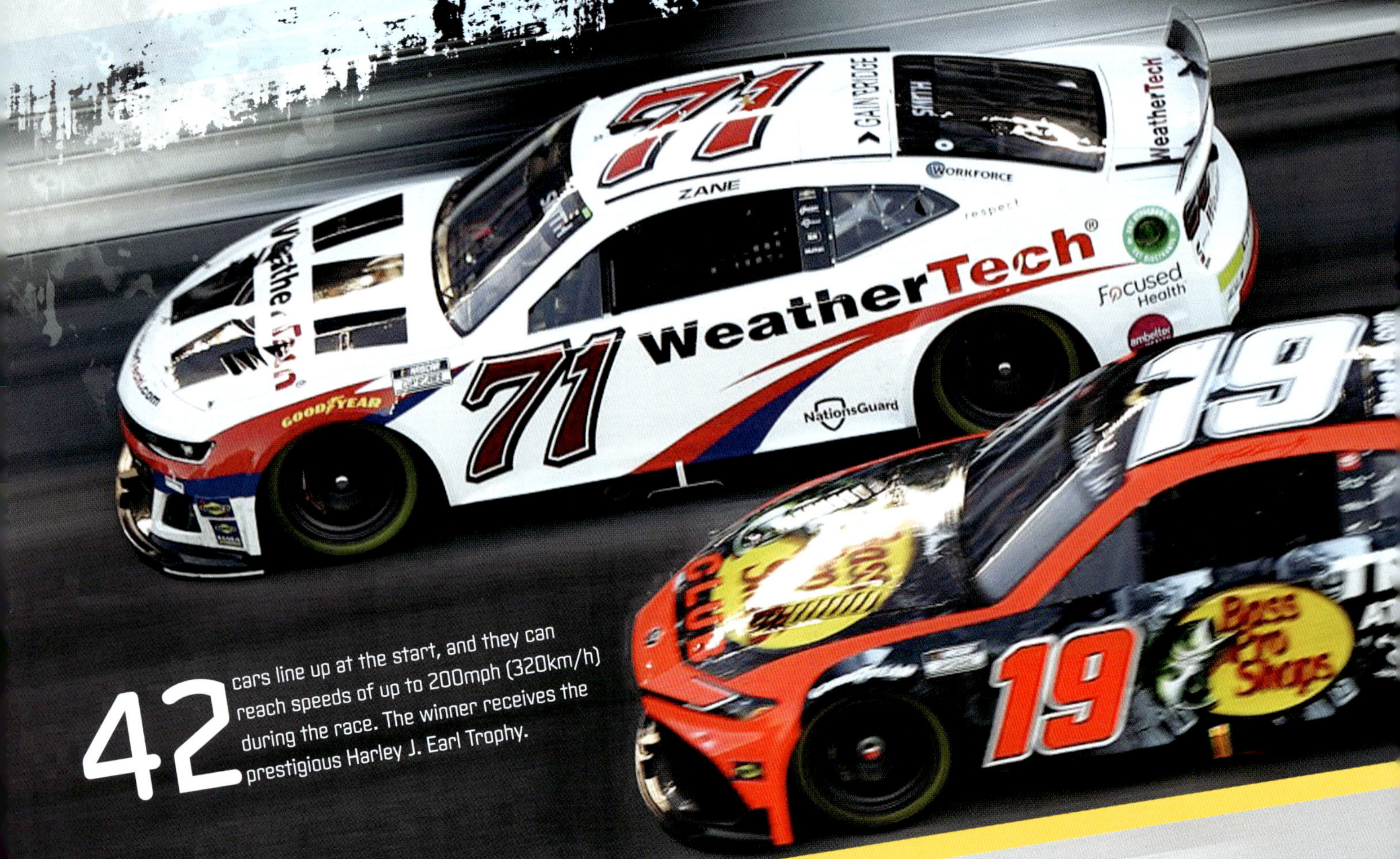

42 cars line up at the start, and they can reach speeds of up to 200mph (320km/h) during the race. The winner receives the prestigious Harley J. Earl Trophy.

THE TRACK

Like most NASCAR races, the Daytona 500 is held on a banked oval circuit featuring all-left turns. As the name suggests, the race is 500 miles long, with cars doing **200** laps of the **2.5 mile** circuit. The race takes around three-and-a-half hours to complete.

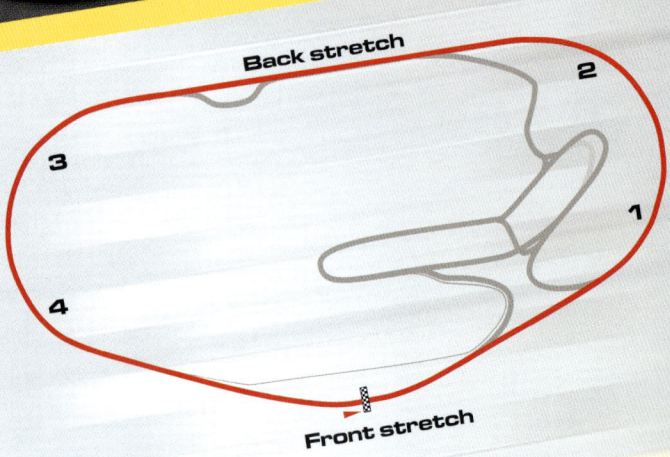

Back stretch
2
3
1
4
Front stretch

RACE FACTS

VENUE: Daytona International Speedway

FIRST HELD: February 22, 1959

LENGTH: 500 miles (804.67km)

NUMBER OF LAPS: 200

MOST WINS: Richard Petty (7)

MAX SPECTATORS: 123,500

GIRL POWER

In 2013, Danica Patrick became the first woman to start the Daytona 500 in pole position. She ended the race in eighth place, the best-ever finish by a female driver.

DAYTONA LEGEND

Richard 'The King' Petty holds the record for the most Daytona 500 wins, with seven victories between 1964 and 1981. He voiced the character Strip 'The King' Weathers in the Disney animated film Cars.

STAR DRIVERS

From the sport's very first champion, Red Byron, to its most recent, Joey Logano, NASCAR has produced some true racing greats. Here are some of its most celebrated title winners.

ROBERT 'RED' BYRON

ACTIVE YEARS: 1949–1951

STARTS: 15

WINS: 2

POLES: 2

TITLES: 1

FACT
Drove with a special brace after injuring his left leg in World War II.

RICHARD PETTY

ACTIVE YEARS: 1958–1992

STARTS: 1,184

WINS: 200

POLES: 123

TITLES: 7

FACT
Known simply as 'The King', his double-century of race wins is 95 more than anyone else's.

DARRELL WALTRIP

ACTIVE YEARS: 1972–2000

STARTS: 809

WINS: 84

POLES: 59

TITLES: 3

FACT
Became a racing announcer for Fox Sports after retiring as a driver.

DALE EARNHARDT

ACTIVE YEARS: 1975–2001

STARTS: 676

WINS: 76

POLES: 22

TITLES: 7

FACT
'The Intimidator' shares the record for most Championship wins (7).

JEFF GORDON

ACTIVE YEARS: 1992–2016

STARTS: 805

WINS: 93

POLES: 81

TITLES: 4

FACT
Drove for Hendrick Motorsports, the most successful team in NASCAR's history.

JIMMIE JOHNSON

ACTIVE YEARS: 2001–present

STARTS: 699

WINS: 83

POLES: 36

TITLES: 7

FACT
Won five consecutive titles from 2006 to 2010 – a NASCAR record.

JOEY LOGANO

The 2018, 2022, and 2024 Cup Series champion as driver of the No. 22 Team Penske Ford.

DEBUT:	2008
STARTS:	587
WINS:	36
POLES:	31
TITLES:	3

FACT Became the youngest NASCAR race winner at the 2009 Lenox Industrial Tools 301, aged 19 years and 35 days.

RYAN BLANEY

Son of former Cup Series driver Dave Blaney, Ryan won the NASCAR Cup Series Championship in 2023.

DEBUT:	2014
STARTS:	350
WINS:	13
POLES:	11
TITLES:	1

FACT Provided the voice for Ryan 'Inside' Laney in the Pixar film Cars 3.

KYLE LARSON

The 23-time Cup race winner is known as a 'wheel man' for his innate ability to control a race.

DEBUT:	2013
STARTS:	374
WINS:	30
POLES:	21
TITLES:	1

FACT Named one of NASCAR's 75 Greatest Drivers in 2023.

CHASE ELLIOTT

Voted 'most popular driver' by NASCAR fans for the seventh consecutive season in 2024.

DEBUT:	2015
STARTS:	330
WINS:	19
POLES:	12
TITLES:	1

FACT Seven of his 19 NASCAR Cup Series race wins have come on road courses.

KYLE BUSCH

One of only two active multi-time champions, Busch ranks ninth in the all-time wins list.

DEBUT:	2004
STARTS:	722
WINS:	63
POLES:	34
TITLES:	2

FACT Recorded at least one win for 19 consecutive seasons (2005–2023).

WILLIAM BYRON

Multiple race wins early in his career have made Byron one of NASCAR's most popular rising st...

DEBUT:	2018
STARTS:	260
WINS:	14
POLES:	15
TITLES:	0

FACT Winner of NASCAR's second-tier Xfinity Series in 2017.

INDYCAR

USA's premier open-wheel* series takes its name from one of motorsport's most famous races, the Indy 500. IndyCar might appear similar to Formula 1 racing, but it has unique characteristics that set it apart, including rolling starts and several oval circuit races.

STRAIGHT-LINE SPEED

The 17-race schedule is made up of superspeedways, short oval circuits, road courses, and street courses. The oval courses enable IndyCar racers to hit top speeds of 240mph (385km/h), faster than anything seen in F1 racing. However, on street courses it's a different story; when IndyCar raced at the US Grand Prix venue in 2019, the cars lost time on corners, and lap times were more than ten seconds slower.

...BLE

...ggest
... ...olis 500 and
NA... ...ola 600 – take place
on ... In 2001, Tony Stewart
mana... ...plete both, flying straight
from ...anapolis to Charlotte to achieve
this remarkable feat. In total, he raced
1,770km (1,110 miles), finishing 6th
and 3rd respectively.

*Describes a race car with the wheels
positioned outside the car's main body.

SPANISH SENSATION

All IndyCars are built with the same chassis, while their hybrid engines are provided by either Honda or Chevrolet. With little difference between them, the cars provide some thrilling, open racing. Eighteen drivers secured Top-5 finishes in the 2024 season, though it was Spain's Álex Palou who came out on top, winning his third title in four years.

ALEX PALOU (Spa) | FIRST RACE: 2020 **| WINS:** 13 **| POLES:** 7 **| TITLES:** 3

STAR FROM F1

British driver Nigel Mansell achieved the remarkable feat of holding the IndyCar and F1 titles at the same time. The 1992 F1 racing champion moved to America to contest the 1993 IndyCar championship, won the opening race at Surfers Paradise, and then won four more races to become champion in his rookie season. Impressively, four of his wins were on oval circuits, which he described as...

"...daunting, frightening, exhilarating, challenging!"

HOW THE RACE WORKS

IndyCar's annual championship featured 43 drivers in 2024, but you will typically see 27 cars on the starting grid of a race. The Indianapolis 500 is the main exception, with 33 cars lining up for the sport's showpiece event.

Rules for qualifying depend on the type of circuit the cars race on:

Oval*

Two consecutively timed laps. Fastest aggregate time secures pole.

Indianapolis 500

Held over two days, starting with four consecutively timed laps. The fastest 12 advance to a 'Top 12 Shootout', which determines positions 7–12. The top six then go in the 'Firestone Fast Six', where the fastest lap time clinches pole.

Street Course

Drivers are split into two groups and given ten minutes to record their fastest lap. The top six cars from each group advance to the next stage, followed by the 'Firestone Fast Six', where the final six drivers compete for pole.

*except Indianapolis 500

THE POINTS ON OFFER

Most races last about two hours. The winner earns 50 points, while 40 go to the runner-up and 35 to the driver in third. The scale goes all the way down to 5 points for any car finishing in 25th place or lower.

At the end of the season, the IndyCar Series champion is the driver with the most points. Consistency is key – 2024 champion Alex Palou (p.61) had just two race wins, but was a regular top-five finisher throughout the season.

BONUS POINTS

POLE: 1 point

LAP LEADER: 1 point

MOST LAPS LED: 2 points

POLE AT INDY 500: 12 points (points on a sliding scale given to next 11 fastest qualifiers)

PIT STOP PRIZE

As well as a drivers' championship, IndyCar runs a championship for the pit crews. The **Firestone Pit Stop Performance Award** awards points after each race based on the shortest average time in the pit lane. The formidable Team Penske, which has won almost everything in IndyCar racing, picked up the title in 2024.

THE CASH DASH

IndyCar held an exhibition race in 2024 offering a US$1 million pay cheque for the winner. Dubbed the Sprint for the Purse, the 20-lap race near Palm Springs in California was won by Alex Palou in 2024.

INDIANAPOLIS 500

One of the most famous races in the world, the Indy 500 dates back to 1911 and attracts crowds of more than 300,000. That's more than three times the capacity of most football stadiums!

Held on a 2.5-mile-long (4km) oval circuit at the Indianapolis Motor Speedway in Indiana in the US, this is the race every driver wants to win. Not just IndyCar drivers, either! In 2017, the two-time Formula 1 racing champion Fernando Alonso interrupted his F1 race season to compete in what he called "the biggest race in the world in terms of adrenaline, emotion, and atmosphere."

PACKED GRID

The Indy 500 traditionally has 33 cars taking part, making it the biggest race in the IndyCar calendar. To accommodate the extra drivers, the starting grid has three cars on each row. Drivers race for 200 laps to cover the 500-mile distance. It takes around three hours to complete, during which time a car will make six or seven pit stops.

190

The average speed in mph (305.7km/h) recorded by winner Helio Castroneves of Brazil in 2021. His race time was 2:37:19.3846.

WINNING WASP

The inaugural Indianapolis 500, held on May 30, 1911, was won by Ray Harroun in his Marmon Wasp car, which he had helped design. The Wasp recorded an average speed of 74.6mph (120km/h).

CRAZILY CLOSE!

In 2024, a record 18 of the 33 starters led for at least one lap. What's more, just 1.5079 seconds separated the top five cars at the end of the race!

MILKY WAY

After taking the chequered flag, winning drivers head to Victory Lane where they lift the Borg-Warner Trophy and celebrate with a bottle of milk! This long-standing tradition dates back to 1936, when Louis Meyer asked for a glass of buttermilk after his victory. Recent winners have poured the drink over their heads, literally milking their celebrations.

INDY LEGENDS

IndyCar racing has produced several motorsport legends. Here we celebrate some of the sport's record-breakers.

IMMUTABLE ICEMAN

New Zealand's Scott Dixon is known as the 'Iceman' for his cool approach, and it's certainly working. A six-time series champion, he has recorded at least one race victory for 20 consecutive seasons and is still going strong!

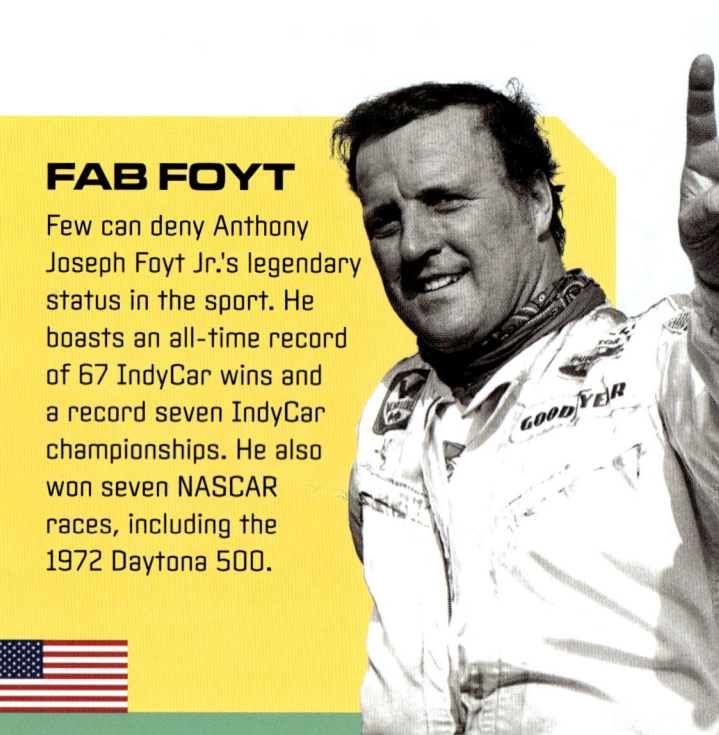

FAB FOYT

Few can deny Anthony Joseph Foyt Jr.'s legendary status in the sport. He boasts an all-time record of 67 IndyCar wins and a record seven IndyCar championships. He also won seven NASCAR races, including the 1972 Daytona 500.

AL'S ACE SEASON

Two drivers have won 10 races in a season: A.J. Foyt in 1964 and Al Unser in his golden season of 1970. Unser led a record 1,527 laps that year (67 per cent of all races) and won more than twice as many championship points as his nearest challenger, his brother Bobby.

DANICA THE TRAILBLAZER

In 2008, Danica Patrick (see p.55) became the first woman to win an IndyCar Series race when she took the chequered flag at the Indy Japan 300 in Motegi, Japan. Patrick has since become an advocate for gender equality in motorsports and a role model for aspiring female athletes throughout the world.

TRIPLE TRIUMPH

Britain's Graham Hill is the only racer to win the 'Triple Crown' in motorsport. He won the Formula 1 World Drivers' Championship title twice (1962 and '68), Le Mans in 1972, and the Indy 500 in 1966.

GO, GO, GO, JOSEF!

In 2024, Josef Newgarden became the sixth and most recent driver to record back-to-back Indianapolis 500 victories. The Tennessee racer is also a two-time IndyCar series winner. He is already considered among the sport's all-time greats in America's top open-wheel series.

CROSSOVER CHAMPS

Four drivers have won both the **IndyCar** and **Formula 1** racing championships:

DRIVER	NATIONALITY		INDY TITLES	F1 RACING TITLES
Mario Andretti		USA	**4** (1965, '66, '69, '84)	**1** (1978)
Emerson Fittipaldi		Brazil	**1** (1989)	**2** (1972, '74)
Nigel Mansell		UK	**1** (1993)	**1** (1992)
Jacques Villeneuve		Canada	**1** (1995)	**1** (1997)

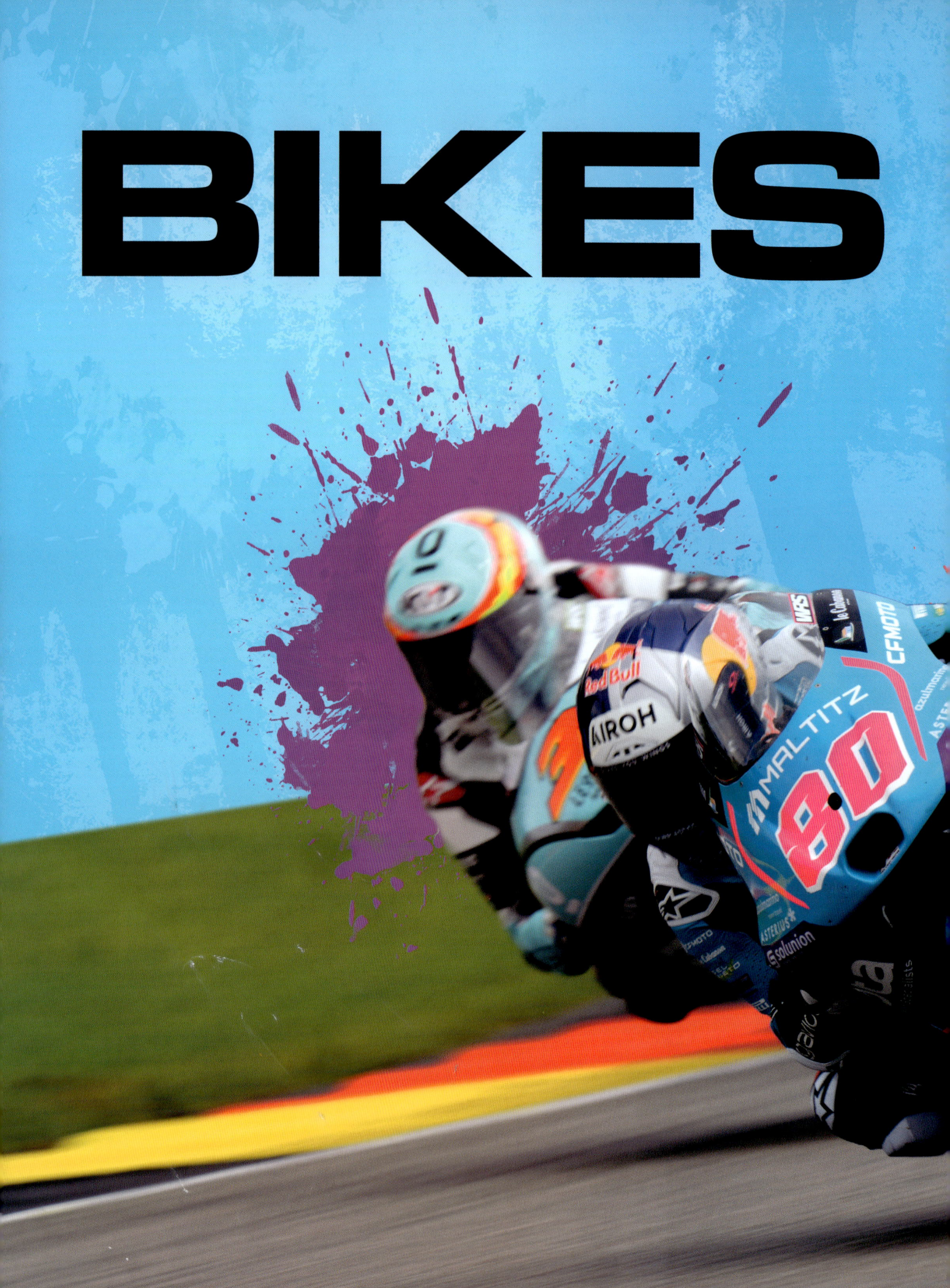

BIKES

Motorsport is not just about four-wheeled vehicles. In fact, bike racing has been wowing international audiences for years. Grand Prix motorcycle racing, which includes the hugely popular MotoGP series, is motorsport's oldest established world championship.

MOTOGP

It takes guts to race motorbikes. MotoGP riders have been clocked racing at more than 350-km/h (218mph) and lean at almost 70 degrees on bends, routinely brushing the tarmac with their knees and elbows while cornering. The 2024 champion Jorge Martín has been known to lean so low that he drags his shoulder on the track. Bikers' exploits have to be seen to be believed!

WORLD TOUR

Over a season, nearly three million fans come to watch MotoGP. The 2025 Championship featured 22 Grands Prix in 18 countries, starting in Thailand in March and ending in Spain in November. Races usually last 45 minutes, but the race weekend lasts three days, with a sprint race held at every meet on the Saturday.

366.1

The top recorded speed in km/h (227.5mph) in MotoGP during an official session, set by Brad Binder in 2023 during the Italian Grand Prix sprint race.

POINTS SYSTEM

The maximum points available in a weekend is 37, awarded when a rider wins both the race and the sprint.

There are 22 riders in a race, with 25 points up for grabs for the winner, plus points are available on a sliding scale for the next 14 finishers.

Sprint races – which are about half the full race distance – offer 12 points to the winner, while the next eight placings receive points on a sliding scale.

In 2023, Francesco Bagnaia won the very first sprint and followed that up with a Grand Prix victory to take maximum points.

RULE ITALIA!

Italy's Valentino Rossi has the most MotoGP race wins (89) and podiums (199), while compatriot Giacomo Agostini has won the most championships (8). Both are legends of the sport.

MOTO2 AND MOTO3

Like most major motorsport championships, MotoGP has junior series to help develop stars of the future.

Moto3 is the smallest class in the motorbike world championship, with bikes using 250cc engines. That's still plenty of power – these bikes can accelerate from 0 to 100km/h (62mph) in under three seconds!

Moto2 bikes are more powerful, using 765cc engines and significantly wider tyres. These classes compete just before MotoGP every race weekend.

THE BIKE

The real stars of MotoGP are the bikes. Costing up to £2.75 million ($3.5m) to build, these machines are supercharged to be the most powerful, efficient machines on two wheels. Let's take a closer look at these speed demons.

LEATHERS

MotoGP riders wear highly protective leather suits. All race suits contain an airbag around the back, shoulders, and rib cage. Sensors in the suit ensure the airbag is fully inflated within 25 milliseconds of a fall!

Knee and elbow sliders are built in for riders to use on corners. The visible hump on the back improves aerodynamics and holds drinking water, which is fed by a tube into the helmet.

CHASSIS

The carbon fibre construction makes the bike lighter and stronger.

WHEELS

The wheels are made out of magnesium, making them lighter than the aluminium alloy used for street bikes.

GEAR LEVER

Rider uses the foot lever on the left-foot peg to perform between 500 and 800 gear changes per race.

ECU

The ELECTRONIC CONTROL UNIT (ECU) is the bike's brain. The various sensors from all parts of the bike send data to the ECU, which makes tweaks based on the information, to help the bike run smoothly.

MOTOGP TYRES

MotoGP bike tyres are slick and grooveless, but provide maximum grip when riders lean into turns. As in Formula 1 racing, riders have a choice of soft, medium, or hard tyres, but they are colour-coded differently. Soft tyres are made of a softer rubber compound that sticks more to the track, allowing the rider to take corners more aggressively, but they deteriorate faster and can actually lose grip when worn. Hard tyres stick a bit less, but last longer.

SLICK TYRES

Soft | Medium | Hard

WET TYRES

Soft | Medium

VROOM!

Bikes in MotoGP are LOUD. Powered by 1000cc engines, the noise from a bike has been measured at 128 decibels. That's louder than a jet plane at take off!

BRAKE DISCS

Carbon brake discs allow a MotoGP bike to go from 300km/h (185mph) to 100km/h (62mph) in about 5 seconds, using only 300 metres of track.

ENGINE

Powerful 1000cc engine purposely designed for MotoGP. It allows bikes to reach speeds of up to 349km/h (217mph). Teams typically require seven to ten engines per rider, per season for racing and testing.

IN 2027, MOTOGP ENGINES WILL BECOME 850CC, FULLY POWERED BY SUSTAINABLE FUEL.

THE CIRCUITS

The MotoGP season features 22 Grand Prix races in 18 countries. Here are some of the standout circuits, chosen for their history, track speed, layout, and ability to draw thousands of fans on race weekend.

LE MANS

Built in 1965, around the famous 24-Hour track, the circuit has been a regular fixture on the MotoGP calendar since 2000.

LOCATION: FRANCE

LENGTH: 4.19KM (2.6MI)

RACE LENGTH: 113KM (70.21MI)

CORNERS: 14

LAP RECORD: 1:29.919 (JORGE MARTIN, 2024)

TOP SPEED: 325.8KM/H (BRAD BINDER, 2023)

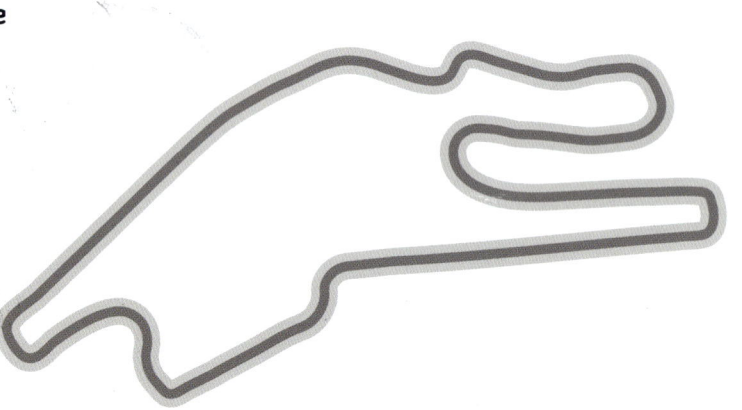

AUTODROMO INTERNACIONAL DO ALGARVE

The stunning 100,000-capacity venue features a circuit with long straights, tight and fast curves, and technical sections.

LOCATION: PORTUGAL

LENGTH: 4.59KM (2.85MI)

RACE LENGTH: 114.8KM (71.33MI)

CORNERS: 15

LAP RECORD: 1:37.226 (MARC MARQUEZ, 2023)

TOP SPEED: 352.9KM/H (MIGUEL OLIVEIRA, 2024)

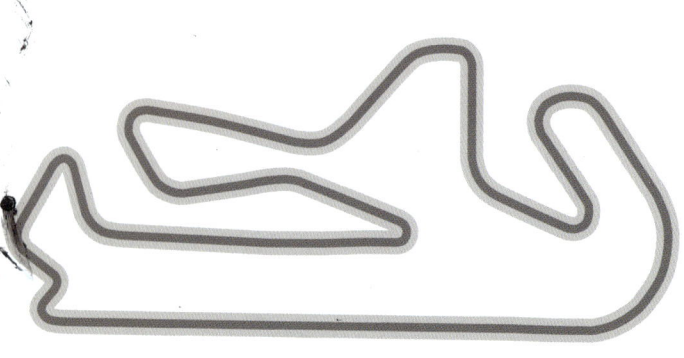

PHILLIP ISLAND

The standout circuit with a challenging layout surrounded by stunning scenery.

LOCATION: AUSTRALIA

LENGTH: 4.45KM (2.76MI)

RACE LENGTH: 120.1KM (74.62MI)

CORNERS: 12

LAP RECORD: 1:27.246 (JORGE MARTIN, 2023)

TOP SPEED: 356.4KM/H (ENEA BASTIANINI, 2022)

MUGELLO

Challenging and popular home of the Italian Grand Prix.

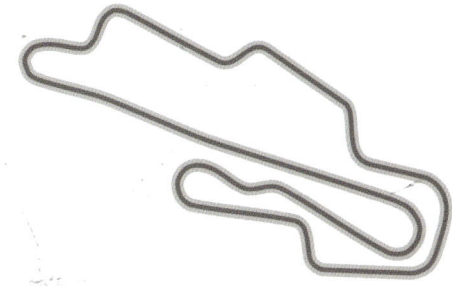

LOCATION: ITALY

LENGTH: 5.25KM (3.26MI)

RACE LENGTH: 120.64KM (74.96MI)

CORNERS: 15

LAP RECORD: 1:44.504 (JORGE MARTIN, 2024)

TOP SPEED: 366.1KM/H (BRAD BINDER, 2023)

SILVERSTONE

The high-speed layout tests the best riders, providing ample overtaking opportunities too.

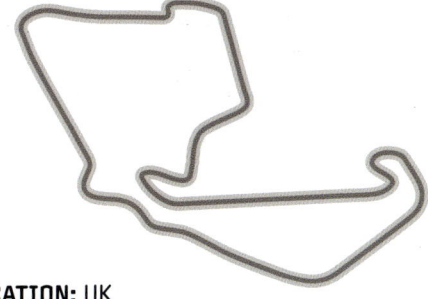

LOCATION: UK

LENGTH: 5.9KM (3.67MI)

RACE LENGTH: 118KM (73.32MI)

CORNERS: 18

LAP RECORD: 1:57.309 (ALEIX ESPARGARO, 2024)

TOP SPEED: 340.1KM/H (BRAD BINDER, 2023)

TT CIRCUIT ASSEN

Part of the MotoGP calendar since 1949, and known for its long straights and fast kinks.

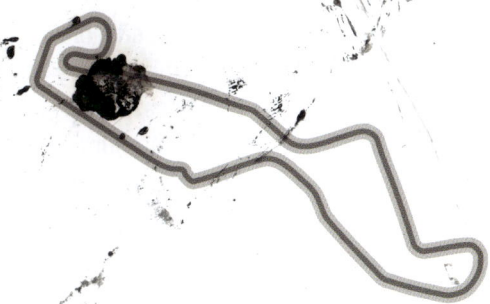

LOCATION: NETHERLANDS

LENGTH: 4.54KM (2.82MI)

RACE LENGTH: 118.09KM (73.38MI)

CORNERS: 18

LAP RECORD: 1:30.540 (FRANCESCO BAGNAIA, 2024)

TOP SPEED: 319.8KM/H (ANDREA IANNONE, 2015)

EASY RIDERS

It takes great skill to get MotoGP's powerful bikes around a track at breakneck speed. Below we break down how riders make those amazing turns, and on the next page we've listed some of today's top riders.

GOING AROUND THE BEND!

Here are three key elements MotoGP riders have to consider when navigating corners as fast as possible.

BRAKING

Knowing when to brake, and how hard, is a key first step. Riders have to apply front and rear brakes at the right pressure, at every turn. Hit them too softly, and the bike is likely to slide off the track. Too hard, and steering becomes a lot trickier.

COUNTER-STEERING

Riders steer in the opposite direction of the turn at first, which helps them lean into it. They retain optimum speed based on the amount of tyre grip they have.

LEANING

Riders judge the radius of the corner and angle their bike accordingly. Finally, they execute the lean and follow the arc of the turn. Their knees and elbows often scrape the tarmac for stability.

JORGE MARTIN

The 'Martinator' won the title in 2024. His super-aggressive style echoes racers from a bygone era.

STARTS: 74

WINS: 8

PODIUMS: 32

POINTS: 1,199

TITLES: 1

FACT Made history as the first MotoGP champion from an independent team.

MARC MÁRQUEZ

The six-time world champion is one of the greatest riders to ever grace the sport.

STARTS: 192

WINS: 64

PODIUMS: 113

POINTS: 3,104

TITLES: 6

FACT MotoGP's youngest-ever world champion (20 years and 266 days, in 2013).

FRANCESCO BAGNAIA

The two-time MotoGP champion won his titles back-to-back in 2022 and 2023.

STARTS: 109

WINS: 30

PODIUMS: 53

POINTS: 1,658

TITLES: 2

FACT Named the 'Comeback King' after he overturned a 91-point deficit to win the 2022 title.

ENEA BASTIANINI

Nicknamed 'The Beast', the Italian racer is renowned for his competitive spirit and racecraft.

STARTS: 72

WINS: 7

PODIUMS: 18

POINTS: 807

TITLES: 0

FACT 'The Beast' won the Moto2 title in 2020.

FABIO QUARTARARO

Arriving in Moto3 aged just 15, Quartararo became France's first MotoGP World Champion in 2021.

STARTS: 114

WINS: 11

PODIUMS: 31

POINTS: 1,146

TITLES: 1

FACT Earned the nickname 'El Diablo' after he wore a helmet with a sticker of a devil on it.

PEDRO ACOSTA

After finishing 6th in MotoGP in 2024, Acosta is looking to build on his impressive debut.

STARTS: 22

WINS: 0

PODIUMS: 5

POINTS: 231

TITLES: 0

FACT The 2023 Moto2 champion is poised for a great future at the top level.

MOTOCROSS

If you like to see motorbikes racing off-road, Motocross is the sport for you. Featuring half-hour races on tricky dirt tracks (mud, grass, or gravel), the sport provides spectacular thrills, spills, and intense competition.

MAJOR CHAMPIONSHIPS

There are two major motocross championships — the AMA Motocross Championship (American Motorcyclist Association) and the predominantly European-based FIM Motocross World Championship (Fédération Internationale de Motocyclisme). Founded in 1972, the AMA Motocross Championship runs from May to August in the USA. The FIM World Championship was first held in 1957, and runs from March to September, featuring rounds in Europe, Asia, and South America. Both now feature two classes of bikes — 450cc (MXGP) and 250cc (MX2).

HOW THEY WORK

The FIM Motocross World Championship is made up of 18 rounds, while the AMA Motocross Championship has 12. Each round consists of two races of 30 minutes, plus two laps in each class. Points from these two brutal races are combined to crown an overall race winner.

INTENSE START

There is no grid in Motocross. Riders line up behind a metal starting gate, with the fastest qualifier choosing their spot first. When the gate drops, it's race time!

The 'holeshot' is what all riders aim for at the start; the word describes the first racer off the starting line who leads the pack into the first corner. This gives the rider a competitive advantage from which they can often control the race. It's a huge part of the race, and the reason riders work hard on their starts.

LEAPING TO VICTORY

Motocross tracks contain several bumps and jumps, and the art of jumping is a key skill in this sport. Here are some of the obstacles riders face on the track:

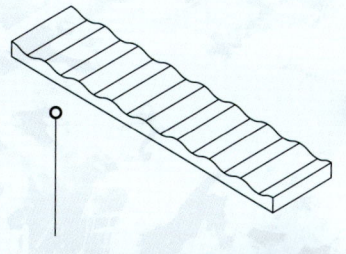

WHOOPS: Small, continuous bumps.

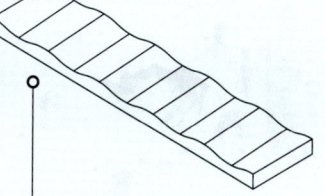

ROLLERS: Rounded bumps in the dirt, larger than whoops.

RUTS: Deep indentations in the track, designed to make the ride tricky.

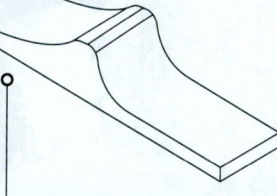

BOOTER: A jump that sends the rider far, rather than high.

RACING PAIR

Motocross isn't just about riding solo. A variation known as sidecross involves racing with the passenger, or 'monkey', leaning out of the sidecar to keep the bike stable.

E-SCOOTERS

Electric scooters have only been around for a few years, and there's already been a sport featuring these vehicles. High-performance E-scooters have staged their own world championship, and it was electrifying!

SUPER SKOOTERS

First staged in 2022, the eSC (eSkootr Championship) season featured six rounds in three continents.

Each round sees 30 riders compete across a series of heats, leading to a final between six racers. Points are awarded in every race and added up over the season to crown the champion.

It's an inclusive series, open to male and female racers. The inaugural winning team included Elise Christie, a world champion short track speed skater.

S1-X RACING SCOOTER

The electric S1-X scooter is all about speed and sustainability. It's built for the racetrack and the future, using state-of-the-art technology. The model comes in varying degrees of power which means it can be used to create a ladder of championships for riders with varying experience.

MAX SPEED: 100km/h (62mph)

LEAN ANGLE: 55 degrees

WEIGHT: 40kg

BATTERY CAPACITY: 1.33 kWh

MAX CURRENT: 200A

ON THE TRACK

Race circuits are around 500 metres long and contain tall starting ramps, bringing excitement from the go. Riders complete several laps, with each race lasting about five minutes.

FRENCH FIRST

France's Aymard Vernay won the inaugural eSkootr Championship, finishing just four points ahead of Italy's Sara Cabrini.

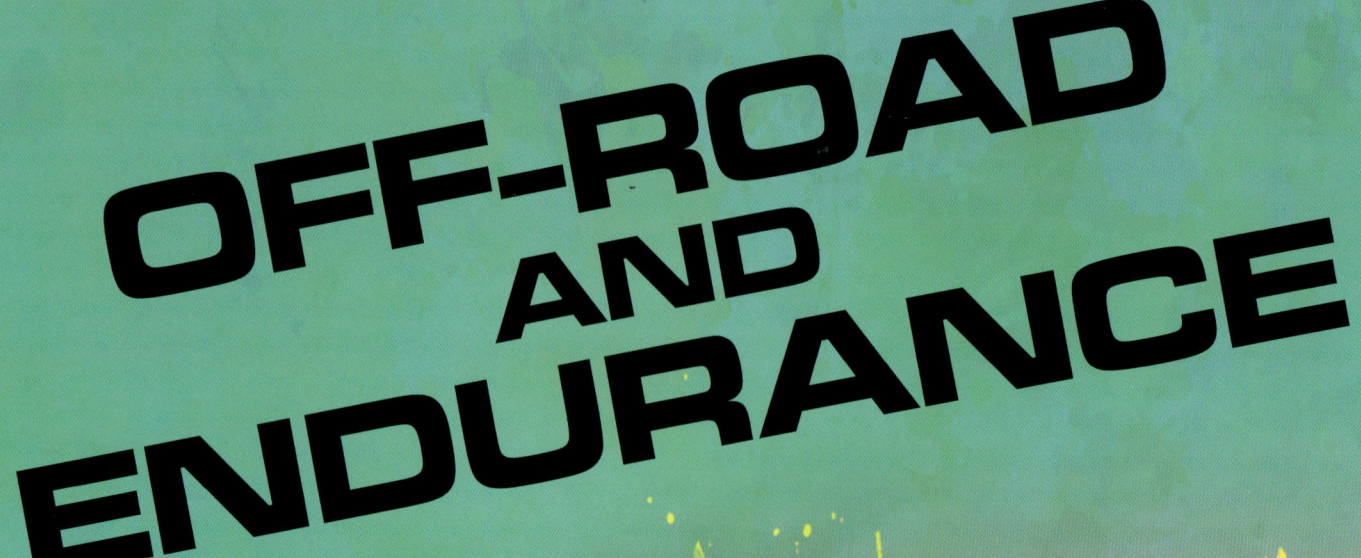

OFF-ROAD AND ENDURANCE

From the famous Le Mans 24-hour race to World Rally Championship stages on mud, snow, and ice, these are the high-profile events around the world that test both cars and drivers to the max.

WORLD RALLY CHAMPIONSHIP

Formed in 1973, the World Rally Championship provides a gruelling test for both cars and drivers. During a season, events take place on treacherous surfaces in extreme temperatures. Which other sport has athletes competing in 42°C (107.6°F) heat and -30°C (-22°F) cold in the space of a few weeks?!

946

The record number of special stage wins by Sébastien Loeb of France, the nine-time champion known as 'Le Patron' (The Boss).

HOW IT WORKS – A 5-POINT GUIDE

1. A WRC event takes place over four days – Thursday to Sunday. Each rally consists of timed courses – known as special stages – on closed roads with surfaces that range from gravel and tarmac, to snow and ice.

2. Usually, between 15 and 25 special stages take place over the four days. Drivers will cover around 300km (186mi) in total.

3. Drivers participate in time trials, tackling the course one at a time at three-minute intervals.

4. The weekend closes with a Power Stage on the Sunday afternoon. The winner of the rally is the driver who records the fastest overall time.

5. A maximum of 35 points are available to the fastest crew: 25 points for the overall winner, five bonus points for Sunday's winners, and another five for the winner of the Power Stage.

PIVOTAL PAIRING

All cars have a co-driver who acts as the navigator, using pacenotes to tell the driver what's coming up. The co-driver maps the route at the start of the week to ensure there are no nasty surprises. They need to be handy mechanics, too.

PATIENT WIN

It took Belgium's Thierry Neuville a record 5,533 days to win his first world title. He made his debut in 2009 and finally became champion in 2024.

CLEAN SWEEP

Gravel tracks can become dirty and slippery overnight, making it tricky for the first car out. This initial drive is known as road sweeping, as it clears the way for the cars that follow. Who goes first? The championship leader. You really have to work hard to become a rally champion!

LEGENDARY LEAPS

Massive jumps, often several dozen metres long, are among the highlights of any World Rally Championship course. The longest jump recorded in a rally car is 85 metres, set by Sébastien Loeb at Rally Turkey, in 2010. Thierry Neuville set the longest distance on the WRC's most famous jump, Colin's Crest at Rally Sweden, with a 44-metre clearance, in 2015.

RALLY LEGENDS

In the early years of the WRC, the cars were the stars. It wasn't until 1979 that we had the first official drivers' world champion – Björn Waldegård of Sweden, driving a Ford Escort. Here, we've picked out a few of the sport's major stars who are part of WRC's exciting history.

SENSATIONAL SEBS

Between 2004 and 2018, two French drivers dominated the championship. Sébastien Loeb won a record nine titles in a row before Sébastien Ogier took over, winning six in a row. They are the two most successful WRC drivers of all time.

MOST WRC TITLES

9 – Sébastien Loeb (France)

8 – Sébastien Ogier (France)

4 – Juha Kankkunen (Finland)

4 – Tommi Mäkinen (Finland)

MIGHTY MCRAE

World champion in 1995, the charismatic Scotsman Colin McRae came close to winning four championships, finishing runner-up twice to Tommi Mäkinen, and then to Richard Burns in 2001. Nevertheless, with 25 career wins, he sits 5th in the all-time list of drivers with the most rally victories.

KID KALLE

Finland's Kalle Rovanperä was just 22 years and a day old when he won the world title in 2022, making him the youngest-ever WRC champion. The son of a former rally driver, he first learned to drive at the age of six ...so was perhaps destined to become the sport's youngest winner.

DID YOU KNOW?

If a car slides off a treacherous track, fans are allowed to help push it back onto the road. In some cases, they tip it back onto four wheels.

CALM KANKKUNEN

Famous for his composure behind the wheel, Finland's Juha Kankkunen was a naturally gifted driver who combined his skill and focus to win world titles across two definitive sets of regulations. After chalking up 23 world rally victories, he entered Dakar (see p.86–87) for the first time in 1988 and won that, too!

DAKAR RALLY

One of motorsport's toughest tests, the Dakar Rally lasts several days. The first started in Paris on 26 December 1978, and ended in Dakar, in Senegal, on 14 January 1979. The event has since relocated to Saudi Arabia and stretches for almost 8,000km (4,791mi).

ALULA
MARATHON

REST DAY
10/01

HAIL

09/01

11/01

08/01

AL HENAKIYAH

13/01

12/01

AL DUWADIMI

RIYADH

14/01

HARADH

FINISH 17/01
SHUBAYTAH

07/01

48H
05 & 06/01

15/01

17/01

16/01

SAUDI ARABIA

BISHA

START

04/01

RE-ROUTING IN 2020

The original route, or Paris-Dakar, as it was commonly known, covered around 9,000km (5,592mi), and took around two weeks to complete. Since 2020, the Dakar Rally has been held in Saudi Arabia. Starting in Alula, it runs from coast to coast, taking in deserts, mountains, and giant sand dunes.

FRENCH FIRST

France's Stéphane Peterhansel is the most successful competitor in both car AND bike. He has won the event a record 14 times – six on a motorbike and eight in a car. Incredible!

RALLY ORIGINS

The Paris-Dakar was dreamt up by Frenchman Thierry Sabine, after he got lost in the desert during another rally. He came up with a motto for his event: "A challenge for those who go. A dream for those who stay behind".

VEHICLES

The Dakar Rally is open to two-wheel and four-wheel vehicles. Besides the Car, there are categories for Bike, Challenger, SSV, Truck, M1000, and Classics (vintage vehicles from previous Dakar Rallies).

SSV

Lightweight 'side-by-side' vehicles with two seats inside a roll cage structure.

BIKE

Built to withstand extreme conditions, powered by fuel-efficient 450cc engines.

TRUCK

Once used solely as support vehicles, 10-tonne trucks nowadays take part in the rally!

BUGGY

Competing in the Challenger class, these light vehicles are fast, even on the toughest terrain.

CLASSIC

Vintage vehicles (pre-2005) from previous Dakar Rallies compete alongside the main event.

ENDURING LE MANS

Held every June in France, the prestigious 24 Hours of Le Mans is the oldest active endurance race in the world. Together with the Monaco Grand Prix and Indianapolis 500, it forms the Triple Crown of Motorsport.

RACE RULES

Cars race for 24 hours, day and night, around a 13.6-km (8.45mi) circuit, reaching top speeds of 330km/h (205mph). Victory ultimately goes to the car that travels the greatest distance in that time!

Each car has three drivers who must rotate over the 24-hour period.

The race starts on a Saturday afternoon and runs through the night, finishing, of course, at the same time the following afternoon.

5410.7

The distance in kilometres covered by the Audi R15 team in 2010 – a race record.

LE MANS LOWDOWN

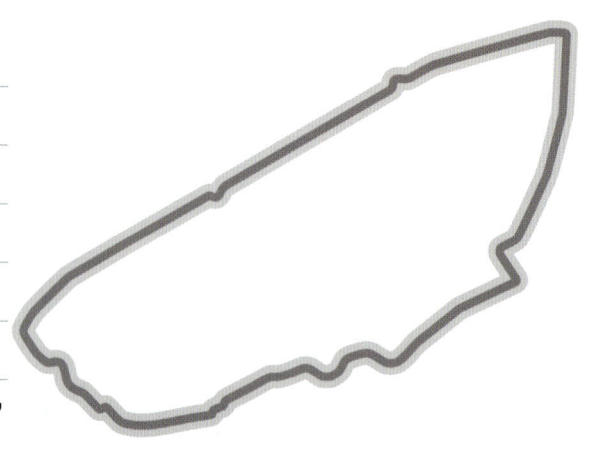

LOCATION: France

ESTABLISHED: 1923

CIRCUIT LENGTH: 13.626km (8.467mi)

MOST LAPS COMPLETED: 397

FASTEST LAP TIME: 3:17.297

SMALLEST WINNING MARGIN: 20m (65.6ft) in 1966

LARGEST WINNING MARGIN: 349.8km (217.4mi) in 1927

A LONG WATCH

More than 325,000 fans attend the 24 Hours of Le Mans race. Some stay for the whole race, which makes it an endurance sport for spectators as well.

SHARING THE DRIVE

To avoid fatigue, a driver is allowed to race for a maximum of four hours at a time. Driver changes happen every few hours when cars refuel or change tyres. Managing the gaps between each drive is an important part of race strategy.

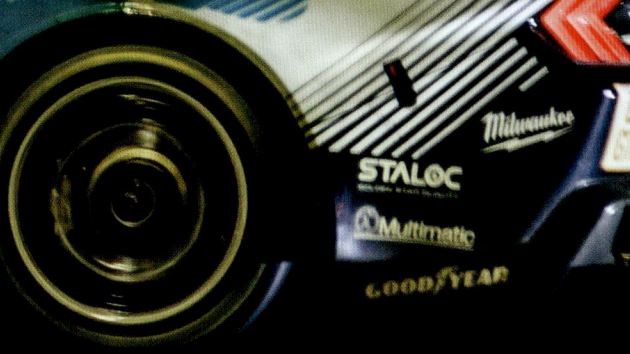

407

The fastest top speed in km/h (253mph) recorded at Le Mans in 1988, set by Roger Dorchy in a WM Peugeot P88, though later advertised as 405 km/h to help Peugeot market the then-new 405 saloon.

EXTREME TEST DRIVE

In the early 1920s, it was the Secretary General of the Automobile Club de L'Ouest, Georges Durand, who came up with a new type of race for France. He suggested something outlandish – a 24-hour endurance race, which would allow manufacturers to prove their cars' worth to potential customers!

FANCY LOT

The 1965, Le Mans' race-winning Ferrari 250 LM fetched a whopping US$36 million (£27 million) when it came up for auction in February 2025!

READY, SET, GO!

Until 1971, the 24 Hours of Le Mans race famously began with a standing start. Drivers would run across the track to their cars, which were lined up in qualifying order on the other side. Known as the 'Le Mans Start', it was eventually replaced for safety reasons, sparked by a protest from the 1969 winner Jacky Ickx.

MOST WINS

DRIVER	CONSTRUCTOR
9 Tom Kristensen (Denmark)	19 Porsche
6 Jacky Ickx (Belgium)	13 Audi
5 Derek Bell (Great Britain)	11 Ferrari
5 Frank Biela (Germany)	7 Jaguar
5 Emanuele Pirro (Italy)	6 Bentley

WORLD ENDURANCE CHAMPIONSHIP (WEC)

The 24 Hours of Le Mans is one of eight events in the FIA World Endurance Championship (WEC), which was created in 2012. Contested across Europe, Asia, North America, South America, and the Middle East, the races vary in length from six to 24 hours. The 24 Hours of Le Mans is the Championship's flagship race!

PHOTO FINISH

In 1966, just 20 metres separated the first two cars. Both were Fords, and the manufacturer had wanted them to cross the line together for a great photo opportunity. In fact, there was only a six-metre gap, and the winning margin was extended to 20 metres when their starting grid positions were factored in.

FAST AND CURIOUS

You can race anything on wheels. Drag racing is so fast, its cars require parachutes to slow down, while lawn mower racing is the ultimate 'grass roots' sport. Buckle up for some of motorsport's most unusual rides!

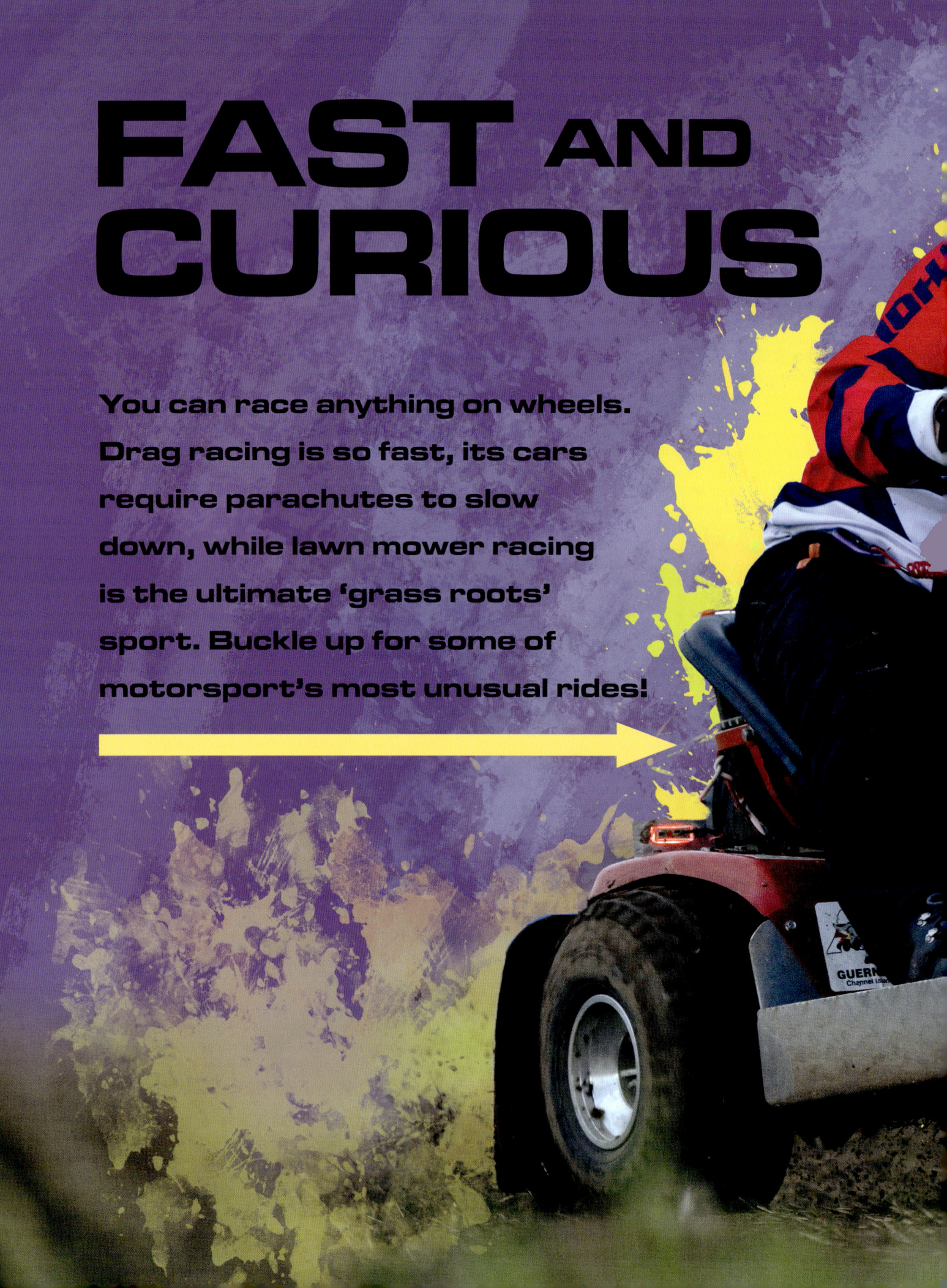

DRAG RACING

Originating in the USA in the 1930s, drag racing is fast, loud, and spectacular. Pairs of cars race against each other over a quarter of a mile (400m), reaching speeds of more than 300mph (483km/h) from a standing start. A race can be over in under four seconds, with the winner progressing to the next round.

PERFECT START

Reaction times are key in a race that happens over a short distance on a straight track. Races are started by a light system known as a Christmas tree (see p.95), and drivers can spend hours perfecting their starts on Christmas tree simulators.

0.8

The number of seconds it takes a Top Fuel dragster to accelerate from 0 to 100mph (161km/h)!

DRAG CHUTES

The National Hot Rod Association requires any car capable of reaching 150mph (241km/h) to have a parachute fitted at the rear, so it can stop quickly and safely after crossing the finish line. Cars that reach 200mph (322km/h) must have dual chutes.

MEAN MACHINES

Drag racing features many different classes of vehicles. Here are some of the standouts.

SUPER STOCK: They may look like regular passenger vehicles but these highly modified cars are built for racing. There is a Stock class, too, where modifications are smaller.

TOP FUEL: Known as the kings of the sport, these dragsters have 11,000 horsepower engines and can reach speeds of 340mph (547km/h). Blink and you'll miss them, although you'll certainly hear them.

FUNNY CAR: These cars mean serious business despite the name. They might resemble a more conventional racing car, and they can reach speeds of 330mph (531km/h).

PRO STOCK MOTORCYCLE: These are bikes, but not as we know them. Highly modified with a purpose-built chassis, these lightweight sprinters can approach speeds of 200mph (322km/h).

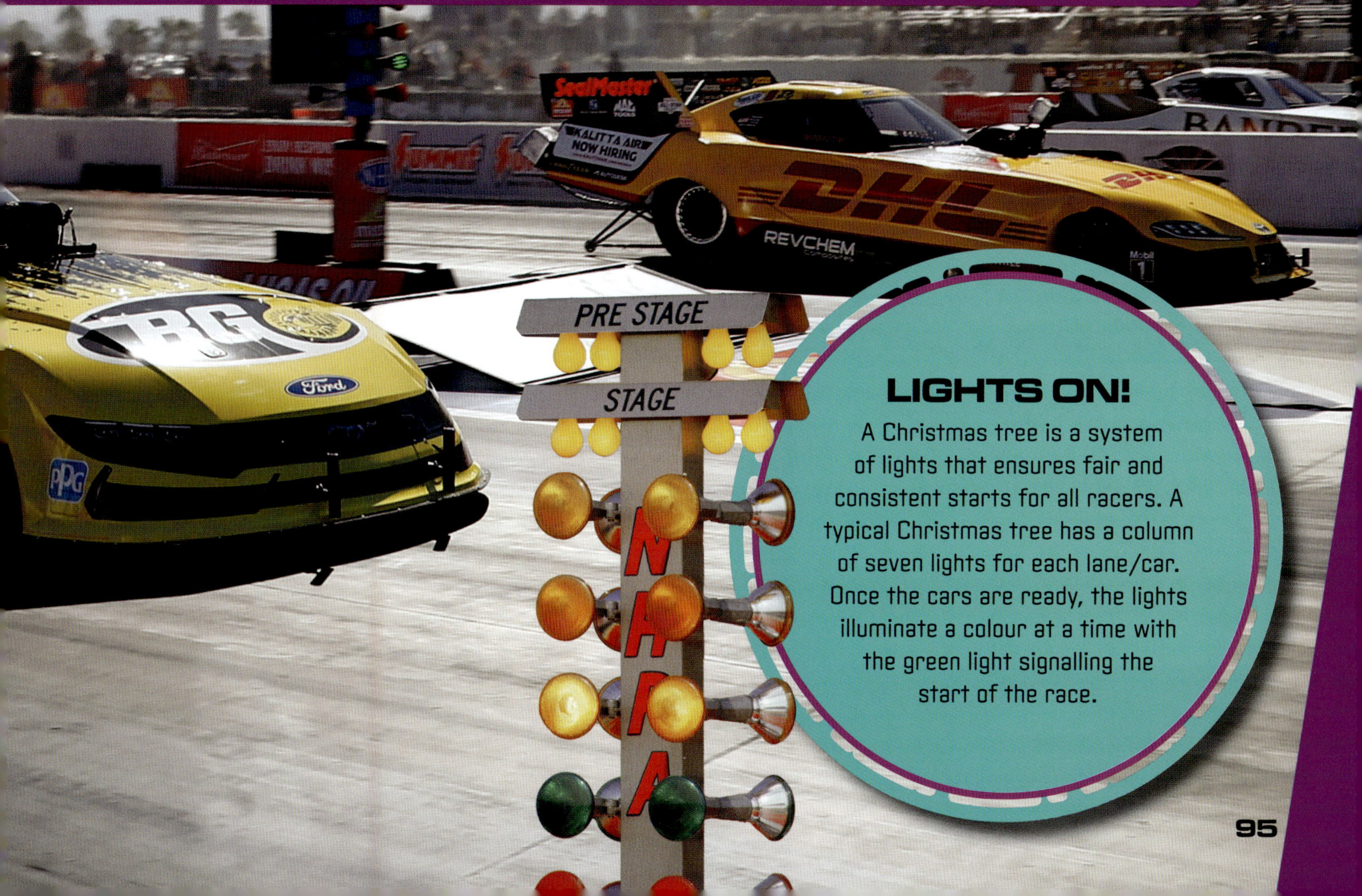

LIGHTS ON!

A Christmas tree is a system of lights that ensures fair and consistent starts for all racers. A typical Christmas tree has a column of seven lights for each lane/car. Once the cars are ready, the lights illuminate a colour at a time with the green light signalling the start of the race.

DEMOLITION DERBIES

There is no racetrack or finish line in demolition derbies. This is a sport where the cars are involved in big hits and smashes, and where crashing is compulsory. The winner is the last one standing.

APPETITE FOR DESTRUCTION

Demolition derbies first became popular in the USA in the 1950s. The cars tend to be old models with sturdy frames – you wouldn't want to smash up a Ferrari. If you are a demolition derby driver, it's probably best not to get too attached to your car.

For safety reasons, windows and windscreens are removed, and doors are fixed shut.

1,000,000

HOW IT WORKS – A 5-POINT GUIDE

1. Most demolition derbies are held on dirt tracks, with a minimum of five drivers per event.

2. When the action starts drivers must register a hit every couple of minutes, or face disqualification.

3. Head-on collisions and deliberate smashes into the driver's door are forbidden. Instead, drivers hit each other tail first, at speeds of up to 30mph (48km/h).

4. Many target the wheels and axles. If a car is unable to move, it's out of the competition.

5. Spray painting the car in bright colours is optional.

WRECK-IT LARRY

Larry Mendelsohn is credited with staging the first modern demolition derby in 1958, after he noticed that fans were more interested in wrecks than racing.

MONSTER TRUCK SHOWS

Known for their super-sized wheels, monster trucks defy gravity with backflips, wheelies, and nine-metre-high-jumps. Shows featuring these vehicles attract more than four million people every year; this is a motorsport that has to be seen to be believed!

SPECTACLE

Most events stage freestyle competitions, where the trucks perform stunts as well as races.

FREESTYLE events involve jumps, flips, and other stunts, which are marked by judges. Among the most spectacular is the front flip – a complete 360 performed by a monster truck weighing around 5.5 tonnes.

RACES involve two monster trucks going head-to-head against each other on a specially designed course with turns. First to cross the finish line advances to the next round.

SAFETY FIRST

Each truck is built with a roll cage, designed to protect the driver at all times. Drivers can hone their skills at a Monster Jam University facility in Illinois, USA.

BIGFOOT

The original monster truck, Bigfoot, was created by Bob Chandler in the 1970s. It began life as a 1974 Ford F-250 pickup truck, but Chandler wanted to make it bigger. And bigger. Before long, a legend was born. There have been several Bigfoots since. In 1985, Bigfoot #5 entered the Guinness Book of Records as the world's largest monster truck, featuring 10-foot (3m) tyres originally used by the U.S. Army.

168

The diameter in cm (66in) of a monster-truck tyre. By comparison, the diameter of a Formula 1 tyre is 67cm (26.4in).

MONSTER JAM

This popular monster truck event brings together the biggest and best of these vehicles. Founded in the 1990s in North America, Monster Jam now tours stadiums and arenas around the world, putting on more than 300 shows every year.

SCORING THE SKILLS

As well as racing competitions, Monster Jam features Freestyle, Donut, and Skills Challenge competitions, where fans get to be the judges. They have 20 seconds after each run to score vehicles out of ten, and use their mobile phones to submit their scores. The skills they vote on include:

BIG AIR
Launching off the Monstergon™ ramp to jump long distances.

BACKFLIP
A complete 360-degree flip using a vertical obstacle.

CYCLONE
A high-speed donut, spinning in circles on the spot.

NOSE WHEELIE
Holding the rear wheels in the air at a 90-degree angle.

POGO
Bouncing on rear tyres while performing a wheelie.

TOP OF THE TRUCKS

Some Monster Jam trucks have earned celebrity status over the years. Here are four fan favourites:

MOHAWK WARRIOR

A cut above the rest, sporting a giant mohawk made of fibreglass broom bristles.

GRAVE DIGGER

Killing the competition for years in freestyle and racing events, now with the formidable Tyler Menninga behind the wheel.

MONSTER MUTT

Dubbed the 'Canine of Carnage' despite its droopy tongue, floppy ears, and waggy tail.

EL TORO LOCO

This raging bull has been winning freestyle titles for more than 20 years.

WORLD FINALS

Known as the Super Bowl of Monster Trucks, the Monster Jam World Finals crown the racing, freestyle, and two-wheel skills champions at the end of each season.

SWAMP BUGGIES

Originally known as 'Tumble Bug', the swamp buggy was built in the 1930s to get through flooded grasslands in Naples, Florida, in the USA. The first official swamp buggy race took place in Naples in November 1949, attracting 50 competitors and a big crowd. Since 1986, races have been held at Florida Sports Park.

MUDDY TRADITION

In 1957, the race winner H.W. McCurry celebrated by throwing his newly wedded wife, now the newly crowned Swamp Buggy Queen, into the muddiest part of the course, still wearing her gown. That tradition survives to this day!

WET AND WILD

Modern swamp buggies have 900 horsepower V8 engines with 68-inch (173cm) wheels, enabling them to power through racetracks submerged in water. The massive wheels can spray water 9 metres into the air during a race!

LAWN MOWER RACING

You can race anything with an engine! This low-budget motorsport has been popular in Great Britain and the United States for half a century. Blades are removed before each race, but fans still believe it's a cut above the rest!

MAGIC MOW-MENT

In 1973, motorsport enthusiast Jim Gavin was having a beer at a pub in West Sussex, England, when he noticed a groundsman mowing the village cricket pitch outside. It's not known how strong his drink was, but that moment inspired the birth of a new sport.

RACING GROUPS

The British Lawn Mower Racing Association (BLMRA) has four racing classes:

GROUP 1
The basic cylinder mower. Push and run!

GROUP 2
Cylinder mower with a towed seat.

GROUP 3
Garden ride-on used for domestic lawns.

GROUP 4
Wheel-driven lawn tractors, capable of reaching 50mph.

FAMOUS WINNER

Stirling Moss – star of Formula 1 in the 1950s - won the British Grand Prix for lawn mowers in 1975 and 1976.

SCHOOL BUS RACING

Swapping the school run for the racetrack, old school buses in this chaotic motorsport are given an unlikely new purpose. Strictly no passengers allowed.

ON A RECKLESS ROUTE

School bus racing takes place on local racetracks in the USA. Some use a figure-8 track, which makes collisions common. Think of it as a route with a crossing that has no traffic lights. On this run, caution flies out the window!

SAFETY LAST

Of the 20 buses that typically compete in a race, around half will ger wrecked. Despite this, safety precautions amount to the use of helmets and seatbelts, but serious injuries rarely happen because of how sturdy the vehicles are.

CLASSIC RIDE

The buses that enter these races are out of commission and typically date back to the 1980s and 90s. Competitors usually buy one at auction for a few thousand US dollars and put their distinctive mark on it.

AUTO RICKSHAW RACING

This three-wheel mode of transport is used by millions of people in south-east Asia. It's not powerful, but it's cheap, reliable, and fun to race.

TUK IT CHALLENGE

In 2020, Red Bull launched a two-day endurance race for auto rickshaws, or tuk-tuks, in Sri Lanka. The event had more than a million views on YouTube, and the series continues to grow – in February 2025 it came to Egypt for the first time, featuring 11 teams and their customised rides!

A SOUND NAME

The vehicle is also known as a tuk-tuk, named after the sound of its small engine.

119

The fastest speed in km/h (74mph) ever recorded by an auto rickshaw. Matt Everard of Great Britain set the world record in 2019 after giving it a new 1,300cc fuel-injected engine.

THE FUTURE

As technology advances at an unprecedented rate, what can we expect to see over the next few years? From AI drivers to the rapid rise of Esports, the future looks green, bright, and exciting.

ESPORTS

Virtual racing continues to grow and shows no sign of slowing down. In 2017, more than 60,000 online racers took part in qualifying for Formula1 Racing's inaugural Esports series. Now known as the F1 Sim Racing World Championship, it features all ten official F1 teams battling for a total prize pot of US$750,000.

E-MAZING DEBUT

At just 16 years, nine months, and 15 days old, Aston Martin's Otis Lawrence is the youngest driver to win in F1 sim racing. The teenager took the chequered flag in the opening event of the 2025 season, on his race debut.

HOW IT WORKS – A 6-POINT GUIDE

1. All 12 rounds consist of a full-length qualifying session and a 50 per cent distance Grand Prix with pit stops.

2. Drivers physically attend each LAN (Local Area Network) event, sitting next to each other in simulators on a stage.

3. Each event features four rounds of racing over three days.

4. The virtual circuits include fan favourites such as Silverstone, Spa-Francorchamps, Circuit of The Americas, and Interlagos.

5. Each of the top-ten finishers scores points, which count towards the F1 Sim Racing Constructors' and Drivers' World Championships.

6. Fans can watch the action on YouTube and other online streaming platforms.

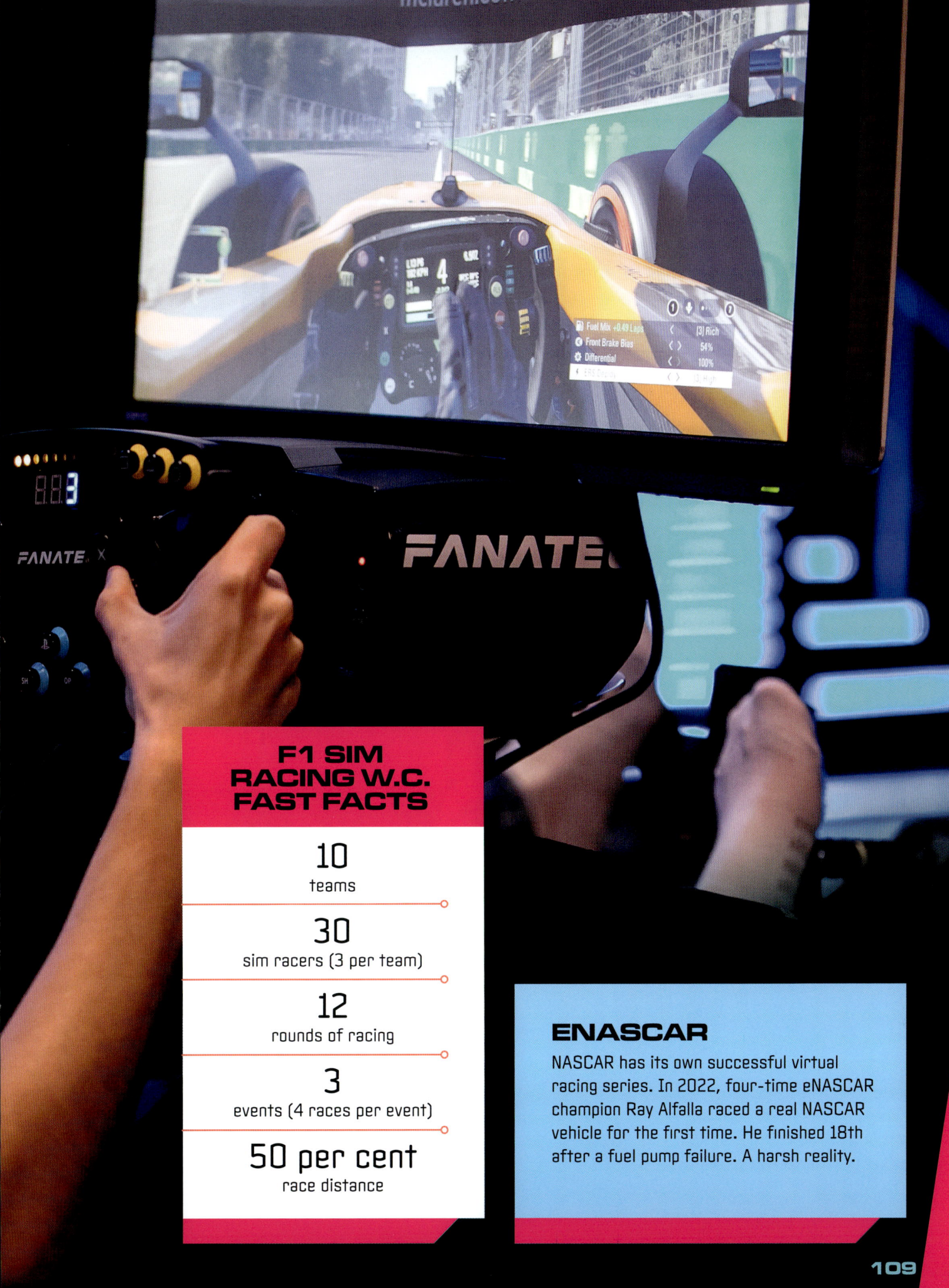

F1 SIM RACING W.C. FAST FACTS

10
teams

30
sim racers (3 per team)

12
rounds of racing

3
events (4 races per event)

50 per cent
race distance

ENASCAR

NASCAR has its own successful virtual racing series. In 2022, four-time eNASCAR champion Ray Alfalla raced a real NASCAR vehicle for the first time. He finished 18th after a fuel pump failure. A harsh reality.

FUTURE CARS

Autonomous racing was trialled in 2024 on the Yas Marina Circuit in Abu Dhabi. All eight A2RL cars were the same; performance was determined by codes created by the teams. Will coders replace drivers as motorsport's biggest names?

FAN-TASTIC ACCESS

Ever wanted to walk on the grid before the start of a race? Or get behind the wheel with your favourite driver? Fan engagement is improving all the time, and these immersive experiences could soon be possible thanks to Virtual Reality (VR) and Augmented Reality (AR).

A driverless car in action on the Yas Marina Circuit in Abu Dhabi in April 2024.

SPIRE

ROBOT RIDER

Yamaha is designing a humanoid robot capable of racing a motorbike. In early test runs it's hit top speeds of 200km/h (124mph) and the MOTOBOT project team is working hard to match the fastest lap times of humans.

TAUGHT BY TECH

AI is transforming driver training. AI-powered simulators are used to mimic real-world racing situations and help drivers practise their skills in a safe environment.

HYDRO POWER

Could hydrogen power the engines of the future? Using hydrogen fuel cells to generate electric power, early models have scored highly on both sustainability and performance.

GOING FOR GREEN

Motorsport is taking big steps to make its future greener. Formula 1 racing has committed to a net zero carbon footprint by 2030, while NASCAR has announced a similar goal.

As part of an initiative to help raise awareness of environmental issues, an F1 car is draped in a huge image of the Earth, instead of advertising and sponsor logos.

GREEN INITIATIVES

▶ 100 per cent sustainable racing fuel

▶ 100 per cent renewable energy at racetracks and team facilities

▶ Remote broadcast production

▶ Ultra-efficient cargo travel between races

▶ Greener travel options for fans

256,551 Formula 1's collective 2019 carbon footprint expressed in tonnes of CO2 emissions. It was reduced by 13 per cent in 2022. Emissions from car fuel made up less than 1 per cent of the total carbon footprint.